Biblical Wisdom to Safely Navigate
the Practice and Honor Your Faith

Christian Girl in the Yoga World

Miranda Jo Davis

STOP
AND READ THIS!

I am sincerely thankful for readers like you! In my gratitude, I would like to offer you a complimentary action guide to enhance the material covered in *Christian Girl in the Yoga World*. My guide, "How to Practice Yoga and Not Compromise Your Faith," uses a simple-to-follow step-by-step format to highlight the top three tips to help Christians find the optimal yoga studio, instructor, or class.

To receive your complimentary action guide, connect here:
https://mirandajodavis.com/book

Dedication

This book is dedicated to my Lord and Savior, Jesus Christ, without whom I would have continued on a hopeless path. Thank You, God, for being the light and love of my life and giving me hope today and into eternity. May this book bring You glory, speak truth, and point others toward Your loving grace.

> "You will know the truth,
> and the truth will set you free."
> John 8:32

Contents

Introduction

Are you a Christian intrigued by the mental and physical benefits of yoga but fearful of trying it because you're concerned about the spiritual roots of the practice?

Are you a Christian who currently practices yoga but is uncertain whether what you are doing is compatible with your faith? Do you love the physical and mental benefits but worry that it might leave you vulnerable to harmful spiritual influences?

If you answered yes, this book is your Christian guiding light for safely navigating the often spiritually dark world of yoga. The truth is, Christian yoga practitioners benefit healthwise but need parameters set in place to shield the mind, body, and spirit. *Christian Girl in the Yoga World* was written to impart wisdom, insight, and accurate instruction to Christians who currently practice yoga or have a desire to start. This book addresses questions, fears, and doubts for readers, as it explores the yoga world through the lens of biblical truth.

With over twenty years of experience as an expert in the yoga industry, I've had plenty of opportunities to investigate both the wonderful benefits and the possible detriments of this practice. My involvement in this profession has resulted in a thriving Christian yoga and Pilates studio, the joy of facilitating global wellness retreats, an E-RYT 500 credential[1] from Yoga Alliance,[2] and many media appearances in television, radio, and print as a top resource for yoga and wellness.

I serve the Lord in ministry as a biblical lay counselor, striving to guide those who need truth and wisdom from God's Word. My understanding of God's truth has been a blessing of abundance, providing opportunities to speak, write, and teach. As a freelance writer and blogger, I have written devotionals, blogs, and articles that have been published in various Christian media outlets such as Proverbs 31 Ministries.

In my time as both a student and a teacher, I have thoroughly enjoyed my years devoted to yoga, as it's afforded me many remarkable experiences. Despite the positive, there have been times when my deepening faith collided with time spent on the mat. I've encountered drawbacks coupled with valid concerns that have made me extra vigilant in my yoga practice. I've experienced firsthand the spiritual danger Christians can face when entering the yoga realm.

I want to equip you to walk the yogic path, but I am also committed to protecting your Christian beliefs. I will shed light on false teaching, pitfalls, and spiritually harmful environments the world of yoga opens the door to.

This book is ideal for

- ❖ Christians who have a desire to begin practicing yoga;
- ❖ Christians currently practicing yoga;

❖ Christians who wish to gain a deeper understanding of yoga's spiritual component;

❖ Christians who are concerned about compromising their faith in practicing yoga.

Christian Girl in the Yoga World includes my testimony interwoven with biblical truth to provide you with confidence on your yoga journey. Each chapter concludes with an opportunity for you to meditate on scriptural truth as well as application questions to help you dive deeper with a self or group study. Heartfelt guided prayers allow you to dialogue with God about specific themes relating to the yoga practice.

Christian Girl in the Yoga World is your modern-day guide to stepping on the mat while honoring Christ and keeping your faith secure. Gain the understanding needed to enjoy yoga while shielding your mind and body from potential spiritual danger!

CHAPTER 1

Stepping onto My Mat and into My Faith

My story with yoga began in 1999, when one of my best friends from college moved to the hippie capital of Texas—Austin—and discovered the practice. During our regular phone conversations and visits, she'd start pitching it. "Miranda, I think you would love yoga. With your dance background, you'd be a natural."

My face scrunched up. I let a blanket of doubt envelop me.

I tried to envision myself sitting cross-legged, eyes closed, index fingers and thumbs connected, but the imaginary smoke from the incense in my visualization drifted in my direction, triggering my sensitivity to smoke and causing a coughing fit.

Nah, I thought. *Not for me.* I dropped the thought like a hot potato.

In the meantime, my personal life was plummeting. Chaos ruled the day, and I had a nagging sense of being unfulfilled, often questioning whether there wasn't more to life than just getting through each day only to do it all over the next. I was hungry for something but had no idea for what. At times my life seemed depleted of joy, and I felt dread mingled with anxiety much of the time.

Ironically, from the outside, my life looked like it was something to be envied as I put on the mask of perfectionism each morning. Despite wanting something more out of life, I felt like I was barely able to keep my head above water. Floundering in the tumultuous sea of life had given me the gift of desperation. I had my eyes open and was ready for someone to throw a life preserver my way, magically pulling me to safer, calmer water so I could feel emotionally and mentally secure.

My health was questionable as well; I'd been diagnosed with irritable bowel syndrome (IBS), a gastrointestinal disorder brought on by stress and poor dietary choices. I felt way too young to spend hours doubled over in pain, having bouts of diarrhea and vomiting. It affected all areas of my life, but at the time I was ignorant of any solutions other than taking medicine prescribed by my doctor.

One day in ballet class, an older woman and I were quietly engaging in conversation while waiting our turn to chassé and pirouette across the floor. I was struggling in class that day after having a bout of IBS and being up most of the night. I confided in her about the battle my body endured the night before, declaring IBS the victor. Her face softened. "Have you heard about yoga?" she asked. I nodded and leaned in closer as she continued. "I have been practicing yoga for many years and believe it could help you."

I drew in a deep breath as I studied the lines of wisdom in her face. She was much older and seemed confident in her statement. "Why don't you think about going to a class?" she continued. At that moment I made a monumental decision. I became willing to give it a try.

Mind you, in the late nineties, yoga was not mainstream like it is today. The search for a yoga class or studio proved to be a challenge, so I felt extremely fortunate to discover a multilevel class at the gym close to my home. I counted down the days in anticipation.

Butterflies filled my stomach as I waited outside the room before my first class. The curvy instructor was blond and sweet faced and amazingly agile for someone at least twice my age. Once we began class, she proved to be a well-seasoned instructor, moving us in and out of a variety of poses like a pro. I could sense my dance background working for me as I confidently made a snap judgment that I was good at yoga.

My grand illusion came crashing down at the end of the class, when the instructor asked us to lie on the floor and breathe. Even though I felt physically tired, taking time to rest was foreign to me. Usually I pushed through everything, so slowing down went against the warp speed of life I was accustomed to.

Her gentle voice encouraging us to breathe and relax was drowned out by the voice in my head: *Why are we doing this? She says to breathe and relax, but am I relaxing? I can't get comfortable. How long are we going to lie here?*

My overactive brain struggled to relax and be still, but because of my type A tendencies, I resolved I would keep going back until I could master the art of doing nothing.

With the seed planted, my love for yoga began to grow. Week after week I went back. Remarkably, I felt better physically, mentally, and emotionally than I had in months. I recognized something that had eluded me quite some time—the ability to experience good health on a multitude of levels.

Yoga helped me on the physical and mental front, but there was a void deep within my soul. Little did I know, another significant life change was just around the corner.

One day after opening my mailbox, I pulled out a flyer for a local church. I studied the pictures of couples and families who looked genuinely happy. Intrigued, I flipped the mailer over to reveal an invitation to join an upcoming marriage series.

My husband and I were newly married and needed some help in the marriage department. After much discussion, he reluctantly agreed to give the marriage series—and the church—a try. So off we went to become part of the most excellent, profound adventure I've ever been privileged to join—my journey to know Jesus.

Attending the first service was a sensational experience. I truly felt welcomed and found it refreshing to see people casually dressed. There was a café for coffee and breakfast snacks, and the worship setting was void of pews, hymnals, and Bibles, which was vastly different from the traditional churches I visited in my youth. But the music sang to my soul, and the pastor's message was Monday-morning relevant. By the time the service came to an end, I knew I was home!

What I did not know was that this was an outreach church, meaning their primary mission was to share the gospel of Jesus Christ and lead people to salvation. Within the first few visits, the pastor invited those of us who did not know Christ to change the course of our lives both here and in eternity by saying a simple prayer while sitting in our seats.

He said, "If you are ready to decide to give your life to Christ, please pray these words with me." My heart raced; I knew it was my time to join the family of God. I sat there quietly while boldly repeating his words. "Today I ask Jesus into my heart to live as my Lord and Savior. I confess I am a sinner and ask for forgiveness of my sins. I believe Jesus died on the cross for me and was resurrected so that I may have eternal life with Him. Amen."

After the words came forth, I felt something shift internally. The Scriptures say the heavens rejoice when one person is saved (Luke 15:10), and although I did not know God's Word or that truth, I do believe that what I felt was a wave of hope wash over my spirit. After feeling empty for so long, I felt fulfilled in Christ. I felt His love, mercy, grace, and goodness welcome me like a long-lost child who had just come home.

It is no coincidence that my coming to believe in Jesus and my journey into the yoga world happened around the same time. I believe that God guided me to yoga to begin healing me from IBS and my type A, high-stress tendencies, but He also guided me to His Son, Jesus, to heal my heart and begin mending the brokenness of my soul caused by sin. Because the truth is, yoga cannot repair our brokenness due to the consequences of sin. Only the power of Christ living within us makes this possible.

Yoga can help curb undesirable behaviors or habits, but it can't do more than that. Merely removing the behavior is like cutting off the top of a weed, leaving the roots to regenerate. Yoga only keeps the behavior in check, whereas Christ exposes the behavior and gets to the root cause.

Take my journey to healing from IBS as an example. Initially it appeared that the illness was primarily due to stress. Practicing yoga helped manage the stress, which helped the symptoms of IBS subside, but not completely. Despite regular time on the mat in practice, my anxiety and stress never fully diminished.

Eventually, in coming to know Jesus, I gained a completely different understanding of my health issue. I discovered that the root of my anxiety intermingled with fear was actually a prevailing sin pattern. I realized I had fears about many aspects of everyday life—fear of not being good enough, fear of failure, fear of people, fear of rejection—and I put my trust in myself, other people, and circumstances rather than the Lord.

I discovered that God's Word had a permanent effect on my spirit, and slowly but surely, faith replaced fear. Putting scriptures like Proverbs 3:5–6 into practice by meditating on and praying over them brought about relief for my anxiety and fear like I had never experienced. This scripture says to "trust in the Lord with all your heart and lean not on your own understanding; in all your ways submit to him, and he will make your paths straight." Trusting God and acknowledging Him in every aspect of my life released me from the stronghold of fear. Anytime fear would try to surface, as it did daily, I would meditate on scriptural truth until I felt comforted and calm.

The gift of living from this perspective has blessed me in more ways than one. Peace and serenity have replaced anxiety and fear, and as a result, my body has experienced complete healing from IBS. Many health struggles for people today are more than physical symptoms; they are generated from reoccurring sin patterns and issues of the heart. In other words, spiritual sickness.

I believed that the Lord had a path set before me and that if my heart would follow His leading, I would be headed in the right direction. Proverbs 3:6 reminds us that not only does God have a path for each of us but He will also keep it straight, putting us back on track when we are prone to wander. This path is for you, me, and every yogi out there who seeks it, giving us blessed assurance we are being led in the right direction.

I believe all Christ-followers are called to take care of our bodies to the utmost of our ability. Part of a believer's path is to be proactive in caring for the body, mind, and spirit.

This is clearly stated in 1 Corinthians 3:16: "Don't you know that you yourselves are God's temple and that God's Spirit dwells in your midst?" It is my experience that many people don't know how to take care of the temple God gave them, resulting in less than favorable health conditions. If we adopted the mindset that a holy, supreme God lives within us, wouldn't we want to make the house where the Holy Spirit resides as desirable and healthy as possible?

If God calls us to treat our bodies as a temple, we must lovingly respond. Yoga can be a beautiful part of seeking to live out health in this realm, but it cannot be the only factor. Yoga can be helpful for our lives, but it cannot be the hope for our lives. Only Christ can.

Yoga can be a stepping-stone for physical, mental, and emotional health, as scientifically proven.[3] Still, Jesus is ultimately responsible for healing the heart and any ailments that may result from being spiritually unwell.

Yoga may bring a lot of bliss, joy, and better things to your life here on earth, but it does not guarantee your citizenship in heaven as believing in Jesus does.

Yoga is a Band-Aid to the soul, bringing temporary relief from pain, whereas Jesus is the surgeon who extracts it completely.

True healing is multifaceted in a Christian's life, with yoga being but one of a gazillion ways our almighty God can bring about healing. Romans 8:28 says, "We know that in all things God works for the good of those who love him, who have been called according to his purpose." If we are called to care for ourselves—to love our bodies and minds that are wasting away daily as we slowly but surely age—then we know that God can take our efforts and use yoga for our good, as I am living proof of!

Scriptural Application

Take a moment to meditate on the truth of God's Word. How can these scriptures help you focus on healing the mind, body, and spirit? How can these verses apply to yoga and help you stay connected to God and His truth?

- ❖ "Trust in the Lord with all your heart and lean not on your own understanding; in all your ways submit to him, and he will make your paths straight" (Proverbs 3:5–6).
- ❖ "I urge you, brothers and sisters, in view of God's mercy, to offer your bodies as a living sacrifice, holy and pleasing to God—this is your true and proper worship" (Romans 12:1).
- ❖ "We know that in all things God works for the good of those who love him, who have been called according to his purpose" (Romans 8:28).

Call to Action: Write for Insight

- ❖ What healing benefits of yoga do you find intriguing? Have you received healing from practicing yoga? Did you credit yoga or God for the healing?
- ❖ Do you believe that God can use yoga to heal your body? Why or why not?
- ❖ What dangers do you think could arise if you put all your faith in yoga for healing and not in God?
- ❖ What sin patterns in your own life do you think could be contributing to health issues? How could you address spiritual sickness (sin) to aid in healing the body?

Prayer: *Dear Jesus, You are the ultimate healer of anything that ails my body. I know You will use whatever You deem necessary in helping me keep my body—Your Spirit's temple—healthy. I want to give You the glory for healing and not credit things made by people. I thank You for the tool of yoga and see its usefulness to my health, but I know ultimately all good things come from You. In Jesus's name, amen.*

CHAPTER 2

Exercising Caution
on the Mat

Several years ago, a movie titled *Couples Retreat* was released. There is a scene where the couples on a marriage retreat take a group yoga class from an attractive, shirtless male instructor played by Carlos Ponce.

The type of yoga he teaches is from a Buddhist-based genre called Tantric yoga. Tantric yoga is described as "a form of yogic practice, which includes sexual and nonsexual teachings designed to transform human consciousness, remove the veils of ignorance, and realize 'enlightenment.'"[4] In the movie the instructor physically adjusts yoga poses of men and women by thrusting his pelvis and genitals on their backsides and inappropriately touching body parts. The spouses watch in horror but, for the most part, say nothing. This movie is a comedy, intended for laughs, making a spoof on Tantric yoga by taking it to the extreme.

However, this isn't a joking matter if something like this has happened to you while practicing yoga. The truth is, the yoga world can be tainted by darkness with physical, mental, or emotional violation taking place. As someone who wants to help you avoid this type of situation in your own practice, I plan to do as Ephesians 5:11 urges by taking no part in this type of darkness but instead exposing it.

Let's look at ways the yoga world creates scenarios that are a clear infringement of the practitioner's mind, body, and spirit.

In the early days of my yoga journey (around 2000), I went to my first large conference in Dallas, where I was practicing with a well-known guru. A sea of yoga mats as wide and long as a basketball court forced me to surrender any illusion of control, as personal space was nonexistent. With a neighbor squeezed in on either side, it was likely their sweat would gravitate to my mat, making this germophobe extremely uncomfortable.

Despite close quarters, I enjoyed the power yoga style,[5] which was new to me. The class was winding down, and with it, so was my energy. Being true to the moment, I decided to gift myself with rest and go into child's pose, a facedown position with the chest draped over the knees and the forehead to the mat.

Suddenly I felt a massive amount of weight distributed across my back, as if someone had just lain down over me. I am small framed and could tell this person was much larger and heavier as he or she deposited every ounce of weight onto my body. I tried to squirm and protest, but I couldn't talk or move as my lungs compressed. I instantly felt panicky and afraid. A female's voice whispered alongside my ear to "be still." What seemed like an eternity of hot, sweaty, full-body contact was, in reality, about twenty-five seconds.

The next thing I knew, she hopped off my back. I quickly looked up to protest, but there were so many instructors and other people moving about, I had no idea who she was or where she went. I tried to wrap my brain around what happened, as I had no experience with anything like this.

Feelings of anger started, but I wondered whether I was overreacting. I tried to reassure myself that surely this famous yoga instructor and his team would not want to harm me or violate my personal space. Still, for the remaining portion of the class, my mind couldn't relax. I kept thinking about what had happened as I silently fumed. In the end, doubt won out, and I didn't utter a word about the physical offense I experienced on the mat that day.

Over the years, I've participated in various trainings on how to respectfully adjust someone in yoga. I learned that, for many reasons, there should never be body-to-body contact. After all, instructors never know whether students are victims of physical or sexual trauma.

Students are in vulnerable positions with their bodies during yoga and believe the space they share with their instructor is safe.

Countless gurus and leaders have been accused or convicted of sexual misconduct, rape, and other abuse of their students in several high-profile cases in the United States. Simply Google "yoga and sex scandals", and a slew of stories appear. Many of the gurus were men who had thousands of disciples, with many of their followers giving everything they had to invest in these leaders. Thankfully, these empires have come crashing down in part, because of movements like Me Too (#MeToo). Even with all that has come to light regarding this type of harmful treatment of yogis, I believe there are countless more untold stories of women or men who have been taken advantage of on the mat.

The bottom line is that people trust their yoga instructors. They look up to them and see their studios as safe places to grow, learn, and blossom in yoga practice. They want truth, love, acceptance, peace, or joy but don't realize these self-proclaimed gurus are sometimes wolves in sheep's clothing.

Jesus warned against something similar in Matthew 7:15–16a: "Watch out for false prophets. They come to you in sheep's clothing, but inwardly they are ferocious wolves. By their fruit you will recognize them."

It is important to both acknowledge and remember that our enemy, the wolf in sheep's clothing, is Satan and that he is the master of making sinful things look appealing. He will divert our attention away from God, Jesus, and the Bible's truth and will make people seem credible, wise, and worthy of being followed.

Success in the yoga realm is often equated with a thriving studio and a huge following of people who wholeheartedly proclaim a leader's teachings as sacred. Yet when we look deeper, many times there is no evidence of spiritual fruit. Certain leaders in the yoga community appear to have the answers, the wisdom, and the knowledge people are looking for, but when you look at their religious ideology, it's not of

Christ. Without Him, there is no real truth, solution, or hope, only a fruitless way of living.

Jesus is the truth, the way, and the life, and no one comes to the Father without Him (John 14:6). If you have set your teacher or guru on a pedestal and have placed your hope in that person, at some point you will be let down by his or her choices or actions. It is crucial to remember that human nature includes sin, making all people fallible. If you turn a blind eye to this truth, it could put you in a position to be taken advantage of mentally, physically, or emotionally. By holding humans in such high regard, we can unknowingly make the instructor a type of god in our lives, which is quite dangerous to our spiritual well-being.

Evidently, with over thirty-six million Americans practicing yoga,[6] people are seeking something. Because of the healing nature of yoga, many who have experienced a trauma of some sort go to yoga for relief. The problem arises when people look to a guru and not to Jesus to facilitate their healing and help them with their pain. People who don't know Christ will believe it is the practice that heals their souls, and many times they think of their gurus as the orchestrating gods of all the healing.

Christians who knowingly subject themselves to teachers with values contradictory to those rooted in Christ should consider this warning in 2 Timothy 4:3–4: "The time will come when people will not put up with sound doctrine. Instead, to suit their own desires, they will gather around them a great number of teachers to say what their itching ears want to hear. They will turn their ears away from the truth and turn aside to myths." We cannot turn away from truth or follow our own desires, because in the end, doing so could come back to harm us. We need to know who it is we are entrusting our bodies to for those hours on the mat, especially their religious values.

As Christians, we need to try to place ourselves in the hands of believing instructors who will maintain our safety. During practice, our bodies are in and out of poses, putting us in vulnerable positions. Please know, I understand that Christian instructors are not above abusive or otherwise harmful behavior, because no one is above sin. However, I do believe those walking with Christ recognize the higher standard we are called to live out, and I hope they will adhere to it as leaders.

Teachers are held in high regard God's eyes, and it would be in your best interests to find a teacher with evidence of biblical values and spiritual fruit. As a student, know your rights. Hands-on adjustments or any touching in class should be okayed by you. Your body is yours, and you have a say. Those who violate your right not to be touched are crossing the line.

It gives me comfort to know that it is not karma (which is false teaching) that will judge the guilty but a just God who will fight for those who have suffered at the hands of another. In regard to yoga, we can rest assured that whatever we may have encountered—whether a traumatizing situation on the mat or false teaching—God will take care of our suffering, if not here on earth, then in eternity. We can trust that our pleas for justice will be heard, as He is a righteous judge.

May we recognize that God can meet our need to be safe and feel protected. With His discerning Spirit, may we intuitively know which instructors are going to nurture our spirits and which ones we are to avoid. Above all else, may our primary teacher be Christ, who is our shelter, haven, and protector and who is forever guarding us against harm.

Scriptural Application

Take a moment to meditate on the truth of God's Word. How can these scriptures help you take precautions in a yoga class against physical, mental, or emotional harm? How can these verses apply to yoga and help you stay connected to God and His truth?

- ❖ "Take no part in the unfruitful works of darkness, but instead expose them" (Ephesians 5:11, ESV).
- ❖ "Watch out for false prophets. They come to you in sheep's clothing, but inwardly they are ferocious wolves. By their fruit you will recognize them" (Matthew 7:15–16a).
- ❖ "For the time will come when people will not put up with sound doctrine. Instead, to suit their own desires, they will gather around them a great number of teachers to say what their itching ears want to hear. They will turn their ears away from the truth and turn aside to myths" (2 Timothy 4:3–4).

Call to Action: Write for Insight

- ❖ If you currently practice yoga, do you unknowingly put your trust in your instructor more than in God?

Do you dismiss his or her religious background, or is this of importance to you? Why or why not?

❖ What are the ways you can protect yourself in a yoga studio against unwanted adjustments or inappropriate touch during practice? What are the ways you can do this biblically?

❖ Perhaps you have been adjusted in a yoga class, and you felt a boundary was crossed. This may not have been sexual in nature, but you did not want to be touched or were surprised by the touch. Did you speak up that you were uncomfortable or that you did not want to receive an adjustment? Why or why not?

❖ Have you ever experienced anything in yoga that made you feel as if you were physically or sexually exploited, harassed, or assaulted? If so, how did you respond? Can you consider talking about it with a professional and making a report against the instructor? Would you consider going to Christian therapy or counseling so you can safely share this trauma with a professional?

Prayer: *Heavenly Father, I pray You would protect me whenever I set foot in a yoga studio. May my body be safely guarded as You watch over me in class. I want to practice yoga with teachers who are of the Christian faith, who will guide me in the path of righteousness for Your name's sake. In Jesus's name, amen.*

CHAPTER 3

My Faith
and Practice Collide

When year eight rolled around in my time as a professional yoga instructor, I was invited by a select few colleagues to study the craft in India. I had topped out in my position as a senior instructor for the company I worked for and was honored to be asked to attend. My motive for going was to explore the roots of yoga and increase my knowledge of the practice for both personal and professional use. In all honesty, my education to this point had become my passion, and I pursued multiple avenues for physical and mental training, but I had received little insight into the historical or spiritual aspects of yoga. I was curious and believed exploring yoga in India would be advantageous for me on a multitude of levels.

I felt this was going to be the journey of a lifetime. I envisioned myself riding on elephants, eating the most excellent vegan cuisine, and practicing pose upon pose while gazing out at the Himalayan mountains for inspiration. One adventure after another trickled through my thoughts as I daydreamed about all the unforgettable moments I was sure to experience as a globe-trekking yogi.

When it came time to depart on the journey, my dear friend, an adviser regarding all things Jesus, gave me a prophetic message. I did not grow up in a Christian home, so I thought of her as a spiritual mama, a person whom God had placed in my life to nurture and grow my faith and with whom I had a special bond. In fact, she befriended me at Texas Christian University, when I was her yoga instructor teaching classes on campus.

My friend's sapphire eyes locked with mine, and I tuned in to the sound of her gentle voice. Whenever she spoke, my ears perked; I was convinced that her direct line to God was static free and that she received clear discernment from the Holy Spirit. Sweet but powerful words flowed, emphasizing the importance of packing my "spiritual things" for this trip. She encouraged me to put on the full armor of God, referring to Ephesians 6. Although my faith was blossoming at a leisurely pace during this season of life, I didn't fully connect the dots when I read the passage she mentioned. Regardless, my daily devotion to scripture, prayer, and Christian meditation led me to the conclusion that God was going to speak a word to me in India.

My friend's prophetic words were like foreshadowing in the ultimate horror movie. Little did I know, I was going to experience an attack on my faith, challenging everything I had come to believe, identify with, and love—challenging my walk with Christ. I would indeed hear from God but not in the way I imagined.

My experience going to the other side of the world—especially to a third world country—was not for the faint of heart. My dreams of seeing bright and beautifully clad Indian people gave way to seeing children on the streets, dirty faced and raggedly clothed, begging. Despite being impoverished, people cheerfully smiled, which momentarily soothed my soul. Upon arrival in the picturesque village of Rishikesh—dubbed the birthplace of yoga—I sat openmouthed, trying to digest all the sights I was taking in. While I sat sipping chai tea, monkeys played, the ever-present cow roamed free, and various languages faded in and out as people walked by me. Our retreat leader, Vinod, a young man whose family originated from the area, emerged to greet us. Despite my weariness from thirty-plus hours of travel, I was giddy.

As Vinod began to fill us in on all things vital for our stay, he casually mentioned he was a Vedic astrologist and would be reading our charts during our visit. Vedic astrology, also known as *Jyotish*, is interconnected with the Hindu religion and teaches that karma is discovered by reading astral light patterns.[7] While everyone else in my group seemed delighted, I found myself uncomfortable with the idea. It brought back memories of times in my life before I became a Christian, when I read my horoscope like it was divine truth … only to later discover it was false teaching.

But despite the bothersome news on Vedic astrology readings, I feigned a smile to try to cover up what I was sure everyone around me could hear—the pounding of my heart.

The next day we hiked to Vashistha Cave alongside the Ganges River to meditate. The cave has high vibrational frequencies, and Hindus consider it a sacred place where one can sense "god." I had to wonder which of the hundreds of gods they referenced. I had already seen countless statues of Hindu deities adorning the city. My spiritual barometer was turned up a notch from the day before, so I started praying.

Upon entering the cave, I noticed a sign written in English instructing people to be silent. I took a deep breath and plopped down on the cold, damp rock. Spiritually, I didn't feel right. My internal alarm was on full alert, and my thoughts scrambled like an old radio set on a staticky station. Although I wanted to bolt, I was frozen—mentally, physically, and emotionally. I pretended to meditate, but I felt a genuine presence of evil that came on me like a dark cloak from behind. The hairs of my neck stood up. I remembered the words of James 4:7b: "Resist the devil, and he will flee." Not wanting to signal to my group that I was having an internal freak-out, I slowly exited the cave into the sunlight, where I felt spiritually safer.

Today I am still uncertain of what actually transpired in the cave, but I know the danger I felt was real, and I knew the Holy Spirit was telling me to flee.

Unfortunately, my time in India as a globe-trekking yogi was one spiritual debacle after another, including fire-cleansing ceremonies to purify our souls, visits to Hindu ashrams to receive blessings from Hindu priests, and practicing yoga while bowing to Hindu deities. God's grace sustained me during this time, as I became ill with a stomach parasite and was often too sick to participate. I firmly believe this was God's provision to give me a way out. My spiritual mama's message encouraging me to put on my spiritual armor to "stand against the devil's schemes" (Ephesians 6:11b) was life changing for me as a believer. I was in spiritual warfare in India, and as I imagined, I was hearing from God ... albeit in the most wearisome of ways.

I desperately wished the two-week stint would come to a close before anything else happened. Even though one other attendee claimed to be a believer in Christ, I didn't feel there was any social support for my faith during the trip. When alone in my room, I clung to my Bible to self-soothe while tears streamed down my face, and I cried out to God for comfort. He gently nudged me to the words of Jesus in John 15:18: "If the world hates you, keep in mind that it hated me first."

My lack of participation, questions during lectures and group study, and avoidance of various spiritual practices led most of my group to become critical of my choices. For the first time in my life, I faced opposition for what I believed.

I was barraged with unwarranted questions and comments. I was told to reconsider the church I attended, because it had made me "rigid in my beliefs." As much as I could not understand their adherence to what I considered false teaching, they could not understand my adherence to my Christian faith. And after the trip came to an end, I was informed that my choices in India put me in jeopardy of losing my position as a global senior instructor.

I had traveled abroad numerous times, appreciating different cultural views, but in hindsight, I was naive about what a trip of this magnitude would do to my spiritual life. Thankfully, this experience gave me the confidence to know I would follow God's truth, whatever the cost.

During one of the hardest times in my spiritual life, God gave me His presence and comfort to take a stand for what I held to be true in Christ. Following Jesus wholeheartedly meant I could not turn a blind eye and partake in the yoga world of spiritually deceptive and hollow philosophy. The trip to India came at a time when I had enough biblical knowledge to discern what was truth versus false teaching. Exodus 20:3 says, "You shall have no other gods before me," and in a country with hundreds of false gods, this scripture could not ring truer.

Perhaps at this point, it could be assumed that my experience is specific to the birthplace of yoga. Although this incident is one of extremes, the need to question yoga's religious undertones is not bound to its Indian homeland. Today yoga has expanded, has become westernized, and is accessible to many populations, which is a good thing mentally and physically, but not necessarily spiritually. More times than not, there is some form of false teaching delivered right to your yoga mat.

Take, for example, my time studying at a yoga teacher training conference in San Diego, early on in my career. I was as green as they get in the yoga world and eager to learn and make my way in the global company. I finally had my dream job traveling for a company that certifies, trains, and teaches in a specific style of yoga. This sought-after position afforded me top-notch education, support, and guidance and the luxury of traveling up to sixteen times a year to see God's world. I selected this company for my own yoga education and eventually to work for because the company followed an exercise-science-based model for instruction, correlating with my college degree.

I was like a kid on the first day of school, sitting cross-legged, front row, pen in hand, ready to engage in the conference. The lecture began as my famous yoga colleague started sharing what I hoped to be profound words of wisdom. Taking notes while hanging on her every word, I suddenly came to a stop in my mind during her presentation. *What did I just hear?*

As if she could read my mind, she repeated the statement. "There are many paths to one God."

Stunned, I looked around and saw several people nod. I repeated the sentence in my mind. *There are many paths to one God.* I even wrote it down and stared blankly at the words. Though I was still a new believer, I was confident I had learned in a church sermon that Jesus was the *only* way to God. But what I was hearing in this lecture was completely contradictory.

Thankfully, the Holy Spirit was at work. John 14:6 took shape in my mind, and I remembered what reigned supreme: "I am the way and the truth and the life," Jesus said. "No one comes to the Father except through me." There are *not* many paths to the one true God. He sent His Son, Jesus, as the only way.

Sadly, deception in the world of yoga can come so easily. One phrase, one word, one idea can confuse Christians just as easily as non-Christians, which is precisely what our enemy Satan would want.

Take warning, my believing friend, as this could easily happen to you—or maybe it already has. Perhaps you've found yourself drawn to yoga as a way to do something good for your body and mind. Maybe you've read some of the thousands of articles touting the health benefits of the practice, and you long to experience them. Maybe the yoga studio you checked out or already frequent seems like a good fit because your BFF loves it and their ratings are stellar. Yet during your search for the perfect teacher or studio, perhaps you forgot one essential factor when deciding whether this space is a good fit for you: Is this yoga teacher or studio a spiritually safe environment for the professing Christian? Will this instructor and environment subtly or overtly push their Eastern religion on you?

Here's the truth: traditional Eastern yoga practice does not separate yoga from religion. Yoga stemmed from the Vedas,[8] Indian holy texts, created around 1500–1200 BC, which form a foundation of the Hindu faith. The word *yoga* itself is a general term encompassing many types. For example, bhakti yoga offers a path to self-realization and advocates a "union through love and devotion" (*bhakti* comes from a root meaning "to adore or worship god").[9] Karma yoga, however, focuses on the holy scriptures from the Bhagavad Gita, claiming it is "one of the paths to purify the mind and ultimately leads to spiritual liberation."[10]

Today westernized yoga is primarily based on the style called *hatha*, which focuses on the physical execution of poses. Many instructors water down traditional philosophy in this type of class but without totally eliminating it.

Yoga is a Sanskrit word meaning "yoking." It is crucial, as Christians, that we ask ourselves whom we want to physically, mentally, and spiritually yoke ourselves to.

Scriptural Application

Take a moment to meditate on the truth of God's Word. In regard to exposing yoga as a link to Eastern religion, what do the Scriptures convey to you?

- ❖ "You shall have no other gods before me" (Exodus 20:3).
- ❖ "Jesus replied, '"Love the Lord your God with all your heart and with all your soul and with all your mind." This is the first and greatest commandment'" (Matthew 22:37–38).
- ❖ "Jesus answered, 'I am the way and the truth and the life. No one comes to the Father except through me'" (John 14:6).
- ❖ "Do not be yoked together with unbelievers. For what do righteousness and wickedness have in common? Or what fellowship can light have with darkness?" (2 Corinthians 6:14).

Call to Action: Write for Insight

❖ Do you think of yourself as a Christian yet find you are open to exploring other religions? If so, why? Do you feel convicted by scriptures such as 1 John 5:21, which says, "Dear children, keep away from anything that might take God's place in your hearts" (NLT)? Does this passage illustrate that God wants to be first and foremost?

❖ Has Eastern religion prevented you from trying a yoga class? Would you try a class if you knew it would be free of false teaching?

❖ If you currently practice yoga, do you find yourself feeling convicted in your class that what's taught is not the truth, yet you continue to go back? Why or why not?

❖ Perhaps you practice yoga but have never been exposed to the religious undertones. How has your yoga practice kept the religious aspect separate? (The instructor, the studio, and the type of yoga you practice are all potential answers.)

❖ Have you ever experienced a yoga class that dove into the religious aspect? How did you respond? Did it compromise your Christian faith?

Prayer: *Dear God, I want to love, honor, and obey You first and foremost. I pray I can safely practice yoga for the wellness benefits and not cross the line of entertaining other religions or false gods. In Jesus's name, amen.*

CHAPTER 4

We Worship
What We Adore

While still in India, I emerged from my room on day five to a crisp, sunny morning, hoping to attain some mental and physical relief for my weary body by joining in a yoga class. The studio we were using was perched above our hotel and had rooftop views of the old village, creating a dreamlike setting. When I walked into the studio, I noticed a sizable sculpture of Ganesha, the Hindu deity known as the remover of obstacles. The statue had the head of an elephant, a human body, and four arms. The way our mats were set up, our bodies faced the statue, creating a sense of uneasiness in my already spiritually tired soul.

The instructor, Vinod, asked us to begin the practice in child's pose, which is a posture of surrender where you are fully bowed down, forehead to the mat, arms stretched forward, and buttocks to your heels. I wondered whether our arrangement had us intentionally bowing down to Ganesha or whether it was just a coincidence. I was leery nonetheless. We started to move, which seemed harmless because it appeared to be only physical movement (or asana), so I began to relax and surrender, allowing stress to exit my body.

About midway through the practice, Vinod asked us to face the deity and chant phrases in Sanskrit, the language of yoga. An internal battle ensued, because I could not speak what I did not believe to be accurate. It took a while to muster the courage to ask what we were saying, and when I did, my question was met with a harsh reply. Loudly enough for everyone else to hear, Vinod said, "You have a huge ego! You need to transcend your ego!" My eyes widened as I gulped back the shame of speaking out. I melted into my mat, facedown, so no one could assess the damage done to my self-esteem.

I've heard it said that *ego* can stand for "edging God out." This was the exact opposite of my intention when I questioned the instructor. Rather than edging God out, I was drawing Him in, clinging to Him as the object of my affection rather than a man-made deity to which to bow or chant. I questioned the instructor because nothing is greater than my adoration for the Creator, and therefore, I had no intention of inadvertently bestowing blessing on a false god.

Worship is natural to human life, happening in the hearts of all people all the time. God created us to worship, and whatever rules our hearts rules our lives. It's vital to realize that worship happens beyond the sanctuary of a church. The dictionary defines it as "the feeling or expression of reverence and adoration for a deity."[11]

First Chronicles 16:23–31 paints a beautiful picture:

Sing to the Lord, all the earth;
proclaim his salvation day after day.
Declare his glory among the nations,
his marvelous deeds among all peoples.

For great is the Lord and most worthy of praise;
he is to be feared above all gods.
For all the gods of the nations are idols,
but the Lord made the heavens.
Splendor and majesty are before him;
strength and joy are in his dwelling place.

Ascribe to the Lord, all you families of nations,
ascribe to the Lord glory and strength.
Ascribe to the Lord the glory due his name;
bring an offering and come before him.
Worship the Lord in the splendor of his holiness.
Tremble before him, all the earth!
The world is firmly established; it cannot be moved.

Let the heavens rejoice, let the earth be glad;
let them say among the nations, "The Lord reigns!"

These verses exalt the Lord, filled with reverence for and awe of the one true King, as He is the only one worthy of our adoration! In a yoga setting, Christians can securely navigate around the pitfalls of yoga if they refuse to worship, bow to, or chant to an inanimate object. In light of 1 Chronicles 16:26—"all the gods of the nations are idols"—it's imperative to remember that in biblical times God's chosen people worshipped metal, wood, or stone—things created by people. This never went well for them, as their sin caused separation from God.

Perhaps you believe this is something that doesn't apply today or in Western culture. Consider this: Have you ever walked into a yoga studio and there to greet you sat a statue of Buddha? Have you ever practiced in a yoga room where some Hindu god was prominently displayed? Perhaps you have witnessed an altar in honor of a deity, but you felt it was the norm since yoga connects to the spiritual.

Because these gods are so commonly seen now, people don't often recognize the meaning behind them or have informed opinions about what they represent. It's as if we are immune to the original context. It is commonplace to see Buddha statues in Target or any other store. Just as a cross symbolizes Jesus and the Christian faith, a Hindu idol represents the Hindu religion, and a Buddhist idol represents the Buddhist religion. Made for worship, these idols are evidence of the beliefs and religious teachings of others, including yoga teachers at the studio where you choose to practice.

Let's bring it back once again to Exodus 20:3— "You shall have no other gods before me"—and apply this to worshipfully moving your body in the presence of idols.

We go to yoga for many reasons. For practicing Christians, it is usually to relax, connect to our bodies, and exercise on a mental, physical, and emotional level. We don't want to go into yoga to mentally and spiritually be on-guard. Studios with idols displayed can introduce elements you may not be prepared to battle.

Unfortunately, it is not only idols we have to be mindful of. We also need to pay close attention to what we absorb mentally and spiritually through our ears. Music is an essential component of the Christian worship experience, just as it is in many styles of yoga. Walking into a yoga studio is a full sensory experience: soothing sounds, dim lighting, serene decor, and the possible aromatherapy infusion or candle. This welcoming combination enhances a worshipful feel, much like church does.

Looking back over the years, I can still see my younger self sprawled on the mat at the end of class, in ultimate surrender. Without a care in the world, I would relish the waves of hypnotic Eastern-rooted music washing over my mind and body. I would zone out, with the sitar and the flute harmoniously conspiring to make sweet sounds interjected with Sanskrit phrases. Having no clue of the lyrical meaning, I was totally ignorant of the words spoken over me.

The years marched on, and just as my walk with Christ deepened, so did my knowledge of yoga. My higher levels of training introduced me to the fascinating language of Sanskrit. I have heard it said that once you have learned something, you can't go back. This was the case for me after beginning to understand this language. I felt like the blinders came off, opening my eyes to what God wanted me to see. As much as I wanted to turn a deaf ear to traditional yoga music, I couldn't go back and unlearn what I believed God was showing me.

Take, for example, a song I've heard countless times in yoga classes, the classical charmer "Om Namah Shivaya." The title translates to "I bow to Shiva," who is one of Hinduism's three primary deities. I think you can see the problem I was discovering!

The jig was up, as I learned most traditional Indian yoga music is written in Sanskrit to worship the founders of yoga and the deities of the Eastern world. Being faithful to Christ meant I could no longer turn a deaf ear to the false teachings sweetly sung over my mind, body, and spirit. My relationship with God was compromised if I continued to savor music advocating untruth.

I have learned I'm not alone when it comes to being cautious about the kinds of music that filter through a class. In fact, one of the questions I get asked often as a teacher pertains to this. A fellow Christian and yoga friend who reached out to me told a tale of being lost in the moment, doing what yogis love—breathing, moving, and connecting—while an ultra-hip, reggae-infused song started up. This New Age style of yoga music gave her a jolt of joy, so after the class she asked the teacher about it. To her surprise, she discovered that the lyrics praised Hanuman, a monkey god believed to invoke devotion in the listener. Unless you researched or understood Sanskrit yourself, you would never know the music was glorifying a false god.

Music often draws the listener in with hypnotic beats and soothing sounds, but the words spoken over you can be deceiving. Philippians 4:8 says, "Whatever is true, whatever is noble, whatever is right, whatever is pure, whatever is lovely, whatever is admirable—if anything is excellent or praiseworthy—think about such things." The keywords in this verse are powerful. Even the music played in a class needs to be true and righteous.

Know what words stream over you in a yoga class. We can't compromise our beliefs for the sake of enjoying a good tune, not when the song proclaims other gods as supreme. We are given freedom in Christ to worship Him but Him only. If you go to a church with sound biblical doctrine and beliefs, you trust that the words spoken are the truth, accepting them as a part of your worship experience. In yoga, we want the same thing.

From a scientific perspective, when practicing yoga, our brain waves change, and because of this, our minds are in a highly suggestive state. You go from your active beta brain wave state to your relaxed, receptive, and meditative theta brain wave state.[12] Much of this has to do with the power of the spoken word.

It's common to hear phrases in some form, encouraging students to "let go," "relax," "breathe," "surrender," "be present," "connect with your mind, body, and spirit." These general phrases are the norm and typically okay in any yoga class.

Christians can be unaware of how Satan uses music and idols to promote the worship of things other than God. We can fool ourselves into thinking, *This isn't that big of a deal*. In reality, this is a huge deal to our Lord and Savior, Jesus Christ. We have to strip away the idea that everything can be justified, overlooked, and made okay because we don't want to believe yoga could be unhealthy for our spiritual lives.

The world thrives on "If it feels good, do it." Instead, we must practice self-discipline and aim to please God above all our selfish desires. As Romans 12:2 says, "Do not conform to the pattern of this world, but be transformed by the renewing of your mind. Then you will be able to test and approve what God's will is—his good, pleasing, and perfect will."

Scriptural Application

Take a moment to meditate on the truth of God's Word. How do these scriptures apply to worship practices in a yoga studio? How can they help you stay connected to Christ?

- ❖ "All the gods of the nations are idols, but the Lord made the heavens" (1 Chronicles 16:26).
- ❖ "Whatever is true, whatever is noble, whatever is right, whatever is pure, whatever is lovely, whatever is admirable—if anything is excellent or praiseworthy—think about such things" (Philippians 4:8).
- ❖ "Do not conform to the pattern of this world, but be transformed by the renewing of your mind. Then you will be able to test and approve what God's will is—his good, pleasing, and perfect will" (Romans 12:2).

Call to Action: Write for Insight

- ❖ When you see an idol or sculpture, do you acknowledge that it is an actual false god, or are you desensitized to seeing these idols?

❖ Have you participated in yoga classes where there were idols present? As a Christian, did you think much about it? How did it make you feel?

❖ Have you participated or would you participate in a Sanskrit chant that repeated phrases glorifying another deity? Why or why not?

❖ If music is played in your yoga class, do you want to know what is said? Do you feel it is okay to be in a class where the music glorifies false gods? Would you tolerate it or have the courage to take a stand for your faith by taking action? Possible actions include having a kind conversation with the instructor regarding your religious beliefs and politely requesting a different style of music (Sanskrit-free). If your request is not respected, prayerfully consider another studio or instructor.

Prayer: *Lord Jesus, I want to obey the first and greatest commandment by loving You with all my heart, soul, and mind. I do not wish to compromise my relationship with You by idolizing false gods. Please help me to be wise and courageous in keeping my commitment to worship You only. In Jesus's name, amen.*

CHAPTER 5

One Chapter Ends; a New Begins

I looked out the giant yoga room windows to the ash-gray sky, a chill going down my spine. Despite the cold February day on the University of North Texas campus, my heart warmed at the thought of leading a yoga certification program over the weekend. I truly love teaching, but after returning from India, I was not finding joy in educating trainees on any curriculum integrating yoga philosophy. My trip revealed that my company and I were spiritually mismatched, and I had been praying about God's will for me regarding the company, specifically whether I was to continue or change paths. Regardless of God's plans, on that day I was all in to teach. In my morning time of prayer, God had reminded me to work as if I did so for Jesus—with excellence and a righteous attitude (Colossians 3:23).

Training days are long and action packed, so it's customary to get students moving after greeting one another at registration. This day was no exception. After the students arrived and introductions were made, we hopped on our mats for the master class, my favorite part of the training.

The master class flowed like poetry in motion, allowing the training to kick off on a high note. At this level of practice, a quicker pace is desirable, encouraging sweat to roll like raindrops from the body. I felt like I was on my A game, teaching to the best of my ability, creating a sense of oneness with each individual. At the close of our practice, I gazed out into a sea of smiling, peaceful people sitting cross-legged on their mats, and I felt at home in my calling as an instructor.

After the class, I dismissed the students for a break and started to shift gears by mentally preparing the lecture portion of the training, my least favorite part. For this, the curriculum incorporated various aspects of yoga's sacred texts, all of which I had come to believe were false teaching. Professionally I knew it was critical to share the traditions, history, and philosophy of yoga because they were key concepts in the training material for this level of certification. I was working for a secular company, so I couldn't just skip or gloss over these ideas. Rather, I sat cross-legged on my mat beneath the fluorescent lights as a nagging sensation formed in the pit of my stomach. The joy and peace I had felt during the practice just moments before gave way to a twinge of anxiety as I pulled out the material to begin the lecture.

Looking at the pages, I drew in a slow breath and quietly exhaled, hoping to appear calm and confident to my waiting students. I plastered on a smile and took the plunge. "Let's begin our journey of Patanjali's Yoga Sutras," I said with as much enthusiasm as I could muster. "Today we will begin by covering the *yamas* and *niyamas*." I saw their faces light up as they opened their manuals. Slowly and mechanically I began to teach the class about Patanjali, a sage who created one of the most authoritative and sacred texts on yoga, called the Yoga Sutras.

These sutras, a Sanskrit word that translates to "threads," outline an eight-limbed path to purify the body and mind, leading practitioners to live meaningful and purpose-filled lives.[13] Followers of the sutras consider them a moral code of conduct and a path to spiritual enlightenment.

Yoga instructors devoted to Eastern philosophy follow the sacred texts as absolute truth. One way they infuse the teachings into their classes is by reading passages from the sutras. They might do so at the opening of class, but more likely, they would share readings while students are in a meditative and highly suggestive state of consciousness at the end of practice in Savasana pose. In this time of quiet relaxation, yogis lie down on their mats to rest. Here, it's customary for instructors to lead guided meditations or share readings.

During the teacher training, I tried my best to educate students from a historical or factual standpoint since I did not apply these teachings to my life. Perhaps you are wondering how that would be possible, so for context and clarification, this is a sampling of what you might have heard if you were a fly on the wall during the training:

> *The first two stops on the eight-limbed path (before getting to the physical postures called asana) are ethical principles geared to guide people in relation to the outside world and themselves. These are the yamas and niyamas, and in the yoga realm, they are said to be something like the Ten Commandments of the Bible.*
>
> *The yamas are things not to do (social restraints), while the niyamas are observances (self-disciplines). Practitioners following the five yamas avoid violence, lying, stealing, lust, and possessiveness; and practitioners following the five niyamas embrace cleanliness, contentment, purification through heat, self-study, and, finally, complete surrender in order to achieve meditative enlightenment or bliss.*

After presenting the information, I encouraged discussion. Their body language, line of questioning, and commentary seemed to indicate many were having light-bulb moments. I could see they were taking it all in as more than commentary, perhaps even as a way of life.

My own inner light bulb began to flicker as I wrestled with my strange feelings. The tinge of angst I hoped would dissipate turned into a gentle nudge from the Holy Spirit. My light bulb finally illuminated, and I heard a still small voice speak the truth: *What you are teaching is made from man, not from God.*

If you don't know God's truth as it is written in His Word, man-made philosophies can seem like transformational nuggets of wisdom. I suddenly recognized that this was exactly what was happening here—and *I* was the one feeding them worldly philosophies! As I looked around at these sweet souls I was shepherding, I realized they were hanging on my every word as if it were divine truth. They were sitting at my feet as I fed them false teaching, gobbling up every bite.

At this moment I recognized there was nothing I could do to reverse the spiritual damage done by what I had just shared with my students. I felt convicted and silently prayed. I prayed for these trainees to one day know and believe the truth and desire to walk with Jesus and claim only His Word as supreme. I completed this training by honoring God and doing the best I could but knew in my heart it was the last training I would complete with this company. My prayers were being answered, and God's direction for my life was becoming clear.

It took several weeks of praying, seeking discernment from wise counselors, and processing to understand where God was leading me with yoga. Based on what happened at the training, I concluded He wanted me to speak biblical truth to others, even from my mat. In time I decided to be a vehicle for God's truth in my teachings; I would stand firm on His Word and not lead others astray with false teaching.

Second Timothy 3:16–17 became the foundation for how I wanted to teach yoga: "All Scripture is breathed out by God and profitable for teaching, for reproof, for correction, and for training in righteousness, that the man of God may be complete, equipped for every good work" (ESV).

The Bible had become all I needed to guide me to make choices and live in alignment with biblical views. I saw it as the authoritative text for living and felt called to have it at the root of any teachings, even in yoga class. Although uncertain how my teaching life would look when I left the secular company, I had faith more would be revealed.

Not long after this training, I submitted my resignation and parted ways with the company. The timing was perfect as I entered a new chapter in my life; as a mother-to-be, I could not sustain the frequent global travel. I also believe that God was giving me a legitimate way out of the worldly teaching method that often conflicted with my beliefs.

In sync with my journey of becoming a new mother, I felt God was creating something new in my teaching career.

An idea came about one day while I was in the shower praying. I had been lamenting to God about how much I loved yoga and was committed to honoring Him while teaching, but I had no idea what that looked like or where to start.

Almost instantaneously, the word *perfect* washed over me. My shower wrapped up quickly, as I had a sense of urgency to make a beeline for my Bible. I started to scour the concordance for the word given to me.

After flying through a few scriptures, I landed on Colossians 1:28: "Him we proclaim, warning everyone and teaching everyone with all wisdom, that we may present everyone mature in Christ" (ESV).

My heart rate doubled as I felt exhilaration rush through my body. Bingo! I now had a clear understanding of God's leading.

I gave birth to my baby boy in early spring of 2009 and launched my business venture, PerfectFit—a Christian yoga and Pilates studio—derived from Colossians 1:28. Moving forward on God's path as a Christian yoga instructor, I decided to proclaim Him, teaching His truths in hope of pointing others toward our perfect Savior, Jesus Christ.

Instructing classes today is a night-and-day difference from my earlier teaching, as I have discovered a newfound freedom. Grounding students in biblical truth during yoga gives them an opportunity to hear the Word and let it speak to their hearts. Moving the body to scripture verses is far more inspiring, encouraging, delightful, peace-filled, and purposeful than moving to any other texts on the earth because doing so illuminates the pathway to God's truth and light.

I believe each person who walks into my space feels the love of Jesus wrap him or her up like a warm blanket. Frequently students comment on how welcoming the environment is, and I smile and nod because I pray that every person attending be brought by God. At the end of each class, I pray over every student as they all rest in a quiet moment of reflection.

Amazingly, God has put students of the Muslim faith, an ex-Wiccan, an abundance of atheists, Christians who are not currently walking with the Lord, and strong, faithful women in my care. I don't force my religion on them; I just let the scriptures do the speaking to their souls and trust that God is doing a work in their hearts. He must be because they keep coming back. Out of my love of Him and yoga, He gave me a ministry I could never have fathomed—one I cherish with all my heart.

Remember the previous section about what a class would look like if I were teaching the Yoga Sutras? Well, I think it only fitting to let you experience the truth I would speak over students today in a class where scripture reigns supreme.

If you were my student, you would hear something along these lines at the end of class during the relaxation/ Christian meditation:

Philippians 4:13 says that I can do all things through Christ, who gives me strength. Let's take a moment to direct our thoughts and minds to this truth.

As you inhale, quietly say to yourself while I say aloud, "I can do all things." As you exhale, say, "Through Christ, who gives me strength." Let's repeat this scriptural affirmation several times as it moves from the mind to the heart. Breathe it in and let it speak to your spirit.

Let's remember that the world will tell you things are not possible. But with God's strength, all things are possible. I can be calm. I can be love. I can be light. I can be grateful. I can be kind. I can be strong. I can be all these possibilities because I am rooted to an all-powerful God who lives within me. Let's take the next few moments to breathe and be still, reflecting on all you can be in Christ!

Finally, Hebrews 4:12 perfectly sums up this aspect of my teaching philosophy: "The word of God is alive and active. Sharper than any double-edged sword, it penetrates even to dividing soul and spirit, joints and marrow; it judges the thoughts and attitudes of the heart." Teaching yoga rooted in

God's word is a radical, life-changing practice for myself, and I have witnessed profound heart change in my participants.

The only religious text written for Christians to rely on and live by is the divinely inspired words God presented to us in the form of the Holy Bible. Nothing can replace it! It is not a hollow or deceptive philosophy created by people but rather words of life-giving power directly from almighty God, bringing real soul transformation and abundant blessings via truth.

The Bible is the only moral compass you need for living, so take caution with teachers who say otherwise. What may sound true often fails miserably when you hold it up to the light of God's truth. What goes in our ears and into our minds is absorbed into our hearts, which must be guarded, for they are the wellsprings of life (Proverbs 4:23).

Scriptural Application

Take a moment to meditate on the truth of God's Word. How do these scriptures illustrate that the Bible is the ultimate guide to living righteously? How can these verses apply to yoga and help you stay connected to God and His truth?

- ❖ "All Scripture is breathed out by God and profitable for teaching, for reproof, for correction, and for training in righteousness, that the man of God may be complete, equipped for every good work" (2 Timothy 3:16–17, ESV).

❖ "Him we proclaim, warning everyone and teaching everyone with all wisdom, that we may present everyone mature in Christ" (Colossians 1:28, ESV).

❖ "The word of God is alive and active. Sharper than any double-edged sword, it penetrates even to dividing soul and spirit, joints and marrow; it judges the thoughts and attitudes of the heart" (Hebrews 4:12).

Call to Action: Write for Insight

❖ Do you believe that the Bible is the only text of truth for Christians to study? Why or why not?

❖ As a Christian, do you think it would be possible to go from reading your Bible and claiming it as truth to slowly becoming accepting of yogic philosophy because of the teachings in a yoga class?

❖ If you are a Christian wanting to practice yoga, how would you respond to being taught yogic philosophy as a guide for right living? Would you consider it a valid guide to life or find it false teaching?

❖ If you are a Christian currently practicing yoga and studying yogic philosophy, do you feel this is being true to your faith? Why or why not?

❖ How would having scripture spoken over you as a vehicle for heart change affect the way you practice yoga?

Prayer: *Thank You, Lord, that I have the Bible to speak truth, wisdom, and insight into my life. I believe that Your Word is supreme and the guide for right living. Please help me not to be tempted by other religious texts that sound good but would compromise my relationship with You. In Jesus's name, amen.*

CHAPTER 6

Pretty Little Packages

When I returned home from India, it took time for me to process my experience, and I found myself with a myriad of questions. *What if I had listened to my travel group in India and left my church home because I bought into their declarations about me being rigid and close-minded? Would my Christian walk have been affected?* Absolutely.

One of the participants in my travel group did walk away from Christ. The only other professing believer on the trip is now an instructor of Vedic astrology.

Colossians 2:8 states, "See to it that no one takes you captive through hollow and deceptive philosophy, which depends on human tradition and the elemental spiritual forces of this world rather than on Christ." In the case of my travel companion, she went from dipping her toe in the water of Vedic astrology to diving in and submerging herself in a pool of deception. We are taken captive by empty, false teaching when we put ourselves in a spiritually vulnerable place. Seeds of darkness can in time take root and grow into a gnarly tree of distortion.

Let's acknowledge that deceit can look like a tidy and seemingly harmless package. When you open this beautifully presented gift, one of two things will happen. You will recognize this gift for what it is—false and misleading—and you will mentally say "No, thank you," rejecting it. Or you will become so enamored by the presentation of this offering that you buy into it, saying yes to its appeal.

Yoga classes can be like shiny, pretty little packages. People love how they feel—mentally and physically—after taking a class. Yoga is highly valuable healthwise, making it appear harmless. Digging deeper (beyond the mental or physical benefits), what happens spiritually when the lid to the practice comes off?

For me, opening the sparkling, irresistible yoga box was more than I bargained for. The outside did not match the inside, as deceit can be a shape-shifter. It may look a certain way one time and then different the next because the aim is to lure you away from God. This happened to me a few years after India, when an opportunity came to pursue a higher level of training known as an RYT 500 credential. It was like a carrot dangling in front of my nose. I was prayerful about this new chapter in my career and did not feel any resistance from God about moving forward, so off I went.

The training center was nestled in the beauty of Denver, Colorado, where a dusting of spring snow settled over the Rocky Mountains, making it the picture-perfect setting to study and practice the craft. This training curriculum centered on our bodies' energetic fields, using techniques to keep the flow of energy in balance. My instructor was incredibly knowledgeable—a veteran in the world of yoga and someone I enjoyed learning from. Her bubbly personality matched her bright pink-and-blue yoga pants.

Although she was yoga knowledgeable, I gathered she was not Jesus knowledgeable. Because she was not integrating religious teachings into our classes, I determined her spiritual preference by her Buddhist tattoo and jewelry.

At this point I had a daily relationship with Jesus, and I was much stronger in my Christian faith than I had been on my trip to India. I devoted time in the mornings to growing in my awareness and understanding of who God is. Scripture shaped my walk with Him, and I spent much of my time in devotions, studies, or lectures. With my faith healthy, I felt comfortable at the class, appreciating the scientifically based teachings.

During the lunch break on the first day of the training, I enjoyed digesting both the material and my food as I gazed out a large picture window. I quietly worshipped God as I sat in awe of the majestic mountains and admired His artistic creation.

After lunch, our class reconvened to settle into a new topic: crystals. I am sure I must have squirmed a little as my trustworthy spiritual alarm rang internally. After a quick introduction to the subject, our instructor directed us to find a partner and begin doing some "energy work" with the crystals.

I asked God to help me, to make it clear whether this was something He didn't want me to do. I also reasoned with Him as to why I thought crystals might not be harmful spiritually.

God, You made crystals, and they are a part of the earth You formed. I know You can utilize anything You see fit as a way to heal. Please show me if this is something contradictory to what it is You want me to do. In Jesus's name, amen.

The instructor had an array of colored crystals of varying sizes set out on the floor. Like any gift charmingly packaged, they seemed to gleam, vying for my attention. Each of us was instructed to pick one and hold it in our hands. If you felt "connected" to it energetically, it was supposedly the preferred crystal for you. Though I was skeptical, to say the least, I selected one based on my favorite color, blue.

The next set of instructions had us putting each crystal on a pendulum, leaving it hanging in the air from a short cord. My partner and I decided that first she would be the student while I practiced being the teacher.

I dangled the crystal over my partner's pelvis. Just as the teacher had told us, the crystals moved when placed over a specific part of the body, making large or small circles, rotating clockwise or counterclockwise. I put the crystal over each area of my partner's body, with little to nothing happening until I came to her chest.

When I dangled the crystal over her heart, a flood of intense emotion came over my body in a gigantic wave. My heart felt shocked by a massive dose of sadness and grief, nothing like I had ever experienced. Stunned, frightened, and shaking, I looked around as tears began to form. I opened my mouth to call for help, but my words choked up.

The instructor caught a glimpse of what was happening, sweetly came to my side, and took hold of my shoulders while

I sobbed. My head shook in disbelief because I knew I had crossed the spiritual line. I sat on the floor, reeling as the emotions ebbed and flowed.

My instructor kindly offered an explanation from her point of view, saying a vortex or channel of energy had opened between my partner's heart and my own, allowing me to feel everything inside this woman. My partner backed this up by telling of her recent years consumed by tragedy, loss, and immense grief.

The whole encounter left me dumbfounded because, in my heart of hearts, I believed God was answering my prayer and giving me clear direction. What looked innocent enough was not so at all. Thankfully, it took only one time to see the truth. I sought forgiveness from the Lord for dabbling in a spiritual realm that put me in over my head. I also asked God to give me wisdom about this mentally and emotionally disturbing experience.

Later, back in my room, I found biblical wisdom in Proverbs 4:23: "Above all else, guard your heart, for everything you do flows from it."

In a world of shiny, pretty little packages, guarding our hearts is one of the ways we put on the armor of God. Let's take a moment to explore how we do this.

Think of a soldier going into battle without his sword. He would be unprotected and at significant risk of attack and injury by the enemy. The same concept applies to Christians practicing yoga. We should not go into a yoga class without adequate knowledge of biblical truth, which is our spiritual sword (Ephesians 6:17). The Word of God is applicable to all aspects of our lives, shielding our hearts and minds as it slays untruth.

Ephesians 6:14 says to "put on the breastplate of righteousness" (ESV). Imagine yourself in a yoga class with a thick, heavy piece of metal guarding your heart. With this protection in place, it will be easier to combat any falsehood hurled your way. If you are fearful of being enticed by yoga's pretty little packages, then guarding your heart is of utmost importance in keeping you on the path of following Christ. A dedicated and intentional prayer life and meditating on His Word daily, hourly, or even moment-by-moment will guard our hearts and minds in Christ Jesus (Philippians 4:7).

In summary, being pulled away from the light of Christ and onto a dark path is a genuine concern for Christians who currently practice or want to practice. We must be biblically wise, discerning, always praying, always on alert, as it says in 1 Peter 5:8: "Stay alert! Watch out for your great enemy, the devil. He prowls around like a roaring lion, looking for someone to devour" (NLT).

The reality is, putting yourself in a vulnerable position will open yourself to the spiritual forces of darkness. The scriptures are clear; there's a spiritual battle going on in the heavenly realms at all times (Ephesians 6:12). We as Christians must be conscious of how our choices and actions contribute to this spiritual battle. I learned the hard way and got a taste of just how frighteningly real this battle is.

The deceit wrapped nicely and presented to you on your yoga mat is directly from the king of darkness. He is always looking for opportunities to pull you away from the King of truth. Because of the ties to Eastern religion, yoga can be the perfect storm for anyone stepping onto the mat. Therefore, it is up to you to guard your heart and allow Christ to clearly direct your steps. The God who lives in you is far greater than the evil one who lives in the world!

Scriptural Application

Take a moment to meditate on the truth of God's Word. How can these scriptures help you stay connected to Christ and His truth amid any deceitful practices yoga introduces?

- ❖ "Above all else, guard your heart, for everything you do flows from it" (Proverbs 4:23).
- ❖ "Stay alert! Watch out for your great enemy, the devil. He prowls around like a roaring lion, looking for someone to devour" (1 Peter 5:8, NLT).
- ❖ The entire chapter of Ephesians 6.

Call to Action: Write for Insight

- ❖ Based on the discussion above, do you believe your walk with Christ can be led astray by taking a yoga class that incorporates "energy work"? Why or why not? How would you respond if a yoga instructor introduced crystals and wanted to integrate them into the class?
- ❖ Have you encountered false teachings or practiced something in a yoga class that made you feel spiritually

uncomfortable? How did you respond? Do you continue to take the class even though you know it may not be honoring to God or your Christian faith?

❖ Would you be able to discern what is false teaching in a yoga class and what is not? Being biblically wise is foundational when it comes to recognizing false teaching. Is this an area you need to grow in?

❖ After reading Ephesians 6, list the ways you can put on the full armor of God in a yoga class.

Prayer: *Father God, I thank You for a spirit of wisdom and discernment. I recognize that certain yoga classes can affect my walk with You. I know the Enemy is looking for opportunities to divert my eyes from Christ and present false teachings. I pray You would increase my knowledge of false teaching and shield me from the lies of the Enemy. I ask You to please give me a courageous spirit to walk away from anything that jeopardizes my relationship with You. In Jesus's name, amen.*

CHAPTER 7

Yoga Instructors
Are People of Influence

I have found yoga to be the one form of exercise that I never grow tired of, always look forward to, and can see myself practicing for the rest of my life. By the spring of 2015, having been an instructor for many years, I was eager to be a student and attend a yoga class instead of facilitating one. With a new studio opening in my area, it was the perfect opportunity.

Hopefully you've gathered by now, trying out different instructors and studios has consistently proved challenging in my yoga journey because I'm protective of my faith. I have come to rely on word of mouth from Christian friends, my connections to other instructors who know my preferences, and prayer to help me discern whom to seek out.

Interestingly enough, the new studio I had decided to check out was named The Temple, hinting at religious undertones. The reviews I found of this space and the teacher (whom acquaintances in the yoga world flock to) were stellar. To my delight, the instructor was experienced and had a long list of credentials. The mat-to-mat-packed room reinforced her reputation, and I could not wait to be one among many learning from her that day.

The class started in a familiar and comforting quiet way, allowing me to breathe and become one with the moment. No matter where or with whom I practice, I invite Jesus to partner with me to protect my mind, body, and spirit. I also ask for wisdom and discernment in regard to the words spoken over me, the type of music played, and any type of spiritual teachings that could contradict my Christian values.

As the class progressed, it was apparent this was a gifted instructor. Her sequences of yoga movements were far from run-of-the-mill. They were unique and engaging, reminding me of a carefully choreographed dance routine.

We were about a third of the way through the class, standing up, legs stretched wide, hands interwoven and clasped behind our backs, bodies sweating while holding "bound extended side angle" pose for what felt like an eternity. When I thought I could not take one more breath and persevere, our instructor shocked me.

"Get that [expletive] out of your body!" she shouted. "Let that [expletive] go! Blow it out of your [expletive]!"

I came out of the pose and looked around. Many of the students were smiling while others looked completely oblivious. Perhaps they were desensitized to the choice words, or perhaps they liked the force of the words.

Mind you, I once spoke the same way, weaving profanity into conversations until God convicted me with Colossians 3:8 by conveying the importance of ridding myself of "filthy language." As a professional in the business, I was trained to speak as such, which meant being extremely mindful of the words used while instructing people. I found it disheartening that the instructor felt the need to add such verbiage to her otherwise enjoyable class. My years of becoming strong in the Lord have made my ears sensitive to harsh language, and cursing interwoven with yoga was a deal breaker for me.

Second Corinthians 6:14 can help Christians choose their yoga instructors: "Don't team up with those who are unbelievers. How can righteousness be a partner with wickedness? How can light live with darkness?" (NLT). Allowing someone to lead you intimately—like in a yoga class—unites your mind, body, and spirit to that person. Therefore, we want children of the light and righteousness—those who have Christlike attitudes and perspectives—to be our leaders, guides, mentors, and teachers. Without Christ in them, darkness will be evident through something as simple as speech.

After doing more investigating, I discovered that this instructor did not walk with Jesus; hence, there was no need for her to be in alignment with Christian teachings regarding speech. These things cannot be rationalized or justified, but in obedience to Christ, we must choose to do what is best for our spiritual welfare and unite ourselves to those who will guide us on the pathway to righteousness.

Over the years I have heard people tell me they continue to go back to a yoga class because they know that their unbelieving instructor is a good person. One Christian acquaintance told me she starts praying whenever her instructor begins her "babble" of Buddhist teachings. "No one else teaches like her. I love her class, and I can't find anyone else who can fill her shoes," she rationalized.

I get that; it is hard to change instructors after you have united yourself to one. Therefore, it can feel comfortable to justify and rationalize going back because you have a relationship. Leaving an instructor can feel a bit like a breakup.

In an ideal Christian world, if Christians had unbelieving instructors, it could be an opportunity for us to minister to them, speak truth to them, or point them to the Lord in order to be the light of Christ and lead them away from darkness. Again, this is ideal in winning souls for Jesus's kingdom.

However, the flip side is also possible. This person you have united yourself to and deemed good could be a source of untruth. Despite being good, he or she still buys into a different religious philosophy than you. I want to be clear—there is nothing wrong with having friends and acquaintances of differing backgrounds and views. The issue arises when this person is your teacher, holding this position of influence in your life. Instructors should bring wellness and add value to your mind, body, and spirit, not detract from them.

Furthermore, 2 Timothy 3:5 warns against such people, stating that they have "the appearance of godliness, but [are] denying its power" and that we are to "avoid such people" (ESV). It is important not to confuse someone's good intentions with godliness.

Appearing to be godly, these good instructors may give back to the community, host fundraisers for charity, teach free classes for those who are in need and can't afford them. They may appear to be great examples of people whom you wish to follow and are likely doing good in this world. But when it comes to spiritually yoking ourselves to them, we have been called to follow scripture and be obedient to the power of Christ. We cannot trade in Christ's best for what is merely good.

In Matthew 7:16, Jesus tells us we will know His disciples by their fruit. People who walk with Christ think and speak about things of Christ. They pray, meditate, and try to follow the ways of the Bible, cultivating spiritual fruit. In Galatians 5:22–23, spiritual fruit is expanded to include "love, joy, peace, patience, kindness, goodness, faithfulness, gentleness, self-control" (ESV). Holding up any yoga teacher's philosophy to scripture gives us insight into whom we are exposing our hearts to.

Following Christ involves denying self, which includes our desires and the "good" yoga instructor who speaks obscenities, false doctrine, or other untruths over you.

Pray for them, minister the truth to them, love them, be light in their lives, and even share the gospel with them, but don't let them have a stronghold over you in an intimate practice such as yoga. If you can't detach from this person, it is probably evidence he or she already has some sort of power over your life—the power that belongs to God.

Scriptural Application

Take a moment to meditate on the truth of God's Word. How can these scriptures give you wisdom in regard to a yoga instructor's influence? How can these verses apply to yoga and help you stay connected to God and His truth?

- ❖ "Don't team up with those who are unbelievers. How can righteousness be a partner with wickedness? How can light live with darkness?" (2 Corinthians 6:14, NLT).
- ❖ "Having the appearance of godliness, but denying its power. Avoid such people" (2 Timothy 3:5, ESV).
- ❖ "You can identify them by their fruit, that is, by the way they act. Can you pick grapes from thornbushes, or figs from thistles?" (Matthew 7:16, NLT).

Call to Action: Write for Insight

- ❖ Do you believe it is okay to practice yoga with someone because he or she is a good person, even though he or she chooses to shun God? Why or why not?
- ❖ If you were practicing yoga with an instructor who used expletives during class, how would you respond? Would you try to overlook it and excuse the instructor's behavior, or would you find it offensive?
- ❖ How can your faith provide an opportunity to witness to someone in the yoga world who needs to hear about the love of Christ? Are you willing to share your faith with a yoga instructor or person in your class?

❖ Do you yoke yourself to instructors and yoga studios that knowingly subscribe to another religion? If so, why?

Prayer: *Dear Lord Jesus, thank You for the opportunity to be light among those who walk a spiritually dark path. I see that my faith can be used for Your good and I pray I seek opportunities to minister to those who are lost. I pray You would make me aware of the instructors who choose to ignore the truth and have hardened their hearts to knowing Christ. I pray they will find salvation and walk with You. In Jesus's name, amen.*

CHAPTER 8

The Pose of Pride with a Twist of Judgment

In my early years of yoga, I kept hearing the phrase *no judgment* in classes. I listened to these words many times as we moved melodically to the New Age music, our heart rates pumping and our bodies working on stretching, strengthening, and holding each pose. I often wondered what exactly *no judgment* meant. One teacher explained it as no judgment of ourselves or of those around us. I quickly learned to try not to look at others in poses and, instead, focused on myself and what I could do versus what I could not. Truthfully, no matter how many times an instructor said this phrase, I still saw students exhibiting competitive, forceful, pride-rooted, and driven behavior. Perhaps yoga touts a *no judgment* mentality, but at the core of it all can be a *look at me* attitude.

In my passion for yoga, combined with my curiosity to see what and how other studios and instructors teach, I found myself on the mat at a power yoga studio that hundreds of people praised.

At this time my older son was in the throes of the terrible twos, and I was scrambling to get out of the house amid a mini meltdown over whether he could have more Cheerios. The Cheerios won, and I came flying into the class with just a minute or two to spare. I plopped my mat down next to an older lady with curly brown hair tied up in a makeshift ponytail.

Settling into the practice, I was enjoying the fact this instructor played no music, which made her teaching style different from mine and was a nice break from the usual *Sesame Street* songs playing in my home.

Another compelling and noted difference was the lack of visual demonstration. In my teaching, I love to stimulate my visual learners by letting my body model the poses I am calling out. This instructor preferred to use the students at the front of the class, whom she deemed advanced, as the illustrators for the rest of the participants.

Finding the present moment and allowing my mind and body to unite, I felt a flood of gratitude at the absence of yoga philosophy, as this teacher and style of yoga focus on the physically challenging aspects of the practice.

The instructor sauntered around the room, inspecting students for any misalignment and making hands-on adjustments. She utilized all the space of the studio, making her authoritative presence known both physically and verbally.

Partly because of her lean yet muscular six-foot-tall frame, she had a somewhat commanding presence. Being a power yoga format, this was boot-camp style at its best. "Down Dog," she would shout, and everyone followed suit. "Up Dog," she barked.

A little before the halfway mark of the seventy-five-minute class, the woman next to me was moving at a snail's pace compared with the rest of us. I was glad to see she was doing what she could—after all, the class schedule said it was a multilevel class, accommodating everyone. I believe yoga is readily accessible to all bodies, and I feel empathy for those who are earnestly trying in their practice. The hardworking lady next to me was no exception.

The next series of poses were standing sequences, involving lunges. Typically, there are modifications given in an authentic mixed-level class, although in this case there were none offered. Trying not to focus on my struggling neighbor was hard because it appeared her knees were bothering her in this type of movement.

The instructor took notice as well and went to her side. I was sure the instructor would give the woman a modification to help her out. "What is wrong?" asked the instructor as the lady labored to get up from a lunge.

"I have a knee injury, and I am having some trouble," the woman replied.

The instructor took another look at the woman and flatly said, "Unfortunately, this class won't be for you. It's for more of an advanced practitioner. You're going to need to leave!"

And that was that. Not an ounce of sympathy, kindheartedness, or gentleness.

My eyes narrowed and I felt my jaw tighten. I knew there were several modifications this woman could have implemented to make her practice doable. My heart sank as I watched her gather her things to leave, head hung low and body language conveying deep discouragement intermingled with defeat.

I wanted to scream out, "Please don't go! Let me help you!" I wanted to shout at the instructor, "This is supposed to be a mixed-level class! Of course, there are poses she can do. It is your job to help her out!" I wanted to have a voice for someone who didn't know she had choices. I wanted to be an advocate for someone who may never step on the mat again.

Not knowing how to respond, I felt maybe I, too, should leave. My eyes darted around the room as if I would find a clear sign. Usually I am one who tries to tune out the world when I practice yoga, and since I just barely made the class on time, I had not taken stock of my fellow practitioners.

I took inventory of the room and noticed shirtless, muscular males in their younger years and slim women of various generations atop the many mats. Without skipping a beat, the class carried on, and it was apparent there were no other novices in the mix. The instructor was catering to a physically fit, advanced crowd.

John 7:24 says, "Do not judge by appearances, but judge with right judgment" (ESV). If this instructor had been using right judgment, she would have been sensitive to her participant's needs, inclusive, and accommodating. There would have been no discrimination based on this lady's ability or age if the class were truly mixed and welcoming to all.

The sin of pride is the root of skewed judgment. When we are rooted in pride and shun humility, we have no encouragement, love, empathy, or compassion for someone unable to measure up to others' expectations. The world applauds pride, and in any typical yoga setting, it festers. There are clues aplenty to how pride surfaces—from flaunting a fit body to having the perfect textbook pose to obsessively staring into the mirror during class.

I, too, have not escaped criticism from my yoga peers. Despite my excellent yoga training, other instructors have judged me for the school of yoga I attended, saying it wasn't "real" yoga since it focused on exercise science and not yogic tradition.

God's Word encourages a different way of approaching life: "Don't be selfish; don't try to impress others. Be humble, thinking of others as better than yourselves" (Philippians 2:3, NLT). Everyone who practices yoga is susceptible to pride, no matter how centered the person is in Christ.

So how do you apply humility when so much of the yoga environment is promoting self? Much of the time, the answer rests with the leader of the practice, the instructor. As discussed, instructors are people of influence, and the words they choose to speak over their students have a tremendous impact. Labeling students based on their ability by saying words like *advanced* sparks pride and can cause division in the class community.

A typical scenario would involve the instructor guiding the students into a pose and saying, "For my advanced students, do this option." The instructor may even point to a student, usually in the front row, and ask that person to demonstrate.

The word *advanced* creates a "game on" response in many students, usually those ready to physically prove themselves. Try being an amused observer as these folks, with grunts and grimaces, try to contort and achieve the ideal advanced pose.

Their alignment may be entirely off, and muscles and joints in their bodies are protesting in pain, but because pride is the guiding force, they display a competitive spirit. For these people, being an advanced student is equated with being the best.

Unfortunately, pride in a yoga class combined with a spirit of competitiveness can have enormous consequences, with injury being the primary one. Pushing yourself beyond your limitations in yoga can be detrimental to your physical, mental, and emotional well-being.

On another note, some students hear the word *advanced* spoken in class and have a battle in their minds because they are critical of themselves. The labeling stirs up feelings of inadequacy, shame, and vulnerability because their bodies are not capable of conforming to an ideal shape or what they perceive to be a perfect pose. Physical fitness may not be a considerable part of their lives, but yoga seems doable and an excellent place to start.

Individuals who lean this way frequently walk out of classes because they believe being an advanced student is unattainable. Others take one class or two but never return because they did not understand that yoga is not about perfection. Whether intentionally or not, instructors are giving their students cues to the practice that are not always in alignment with its "no judgment" proclamation. Labeling students is judging them, creating an environment that is not mentally, physically, and spiritually healthy. You feel either better than or less than your peers and not on equal footing with them.

One of the biggest evidences of pride that I have witnessed is in the hot yoga world. In the last few years, however, I have really come to appreciate hot yoga (a room heated to between 90 and 105 degrees) in my time of personal practice. I love the excessive sweating (a wonderful way to boost the lymphatic system), it's a good workout physically and mentally, and there is plenty of deep stretching. What I enjoy most is that the hot yoga studios I have frequented are free from philosophical teachings. *But* hot yoga does present its own set of issues, especially pride.

In the hot yoga environment, attendees tend to be on the younger side or very fit for their age, and for the most part, all participants look like they are physically in shape. It is easy to see how some of these participants are quite proud of their physiques and have no problem showcasing them.

With the studio environment being extremely hot, once you get moving, pools of sweat collect on and around your yoga mat. For this reason, whenever I attend, I choose a space next to the mirrored wall, allowing me to have only one sweaty person beside me.

When the class is in full swing, it takes all the strength you can muster to make it from pose to pose as you draw breath slowly and consciously. For the safety of your body, it is of utmost importance to continually monitor yourself to make sure you are not becoming overheated or otherwise jeopardizing your health. I often check in by using the mirrors. If my face is too flushed, I know I need to slow down, rest, or take a hydration break.

To my astonishment, more times than not, someone around me is taking advantage of the mirrors as well but for different reasons—usually to obsessively study himself or herself. Standing sequences, balance work, seated flows, or twisting creates the intense desire to inspect oneself from head to toe.

Mirrors in a yoga room are intended for positive purposes but can be a distraction for self-absorbed individuals. I have witnessed people trying to sneak selfies of themselves with the help of the mirror despite the "no camera" policy most studios try to enforce.

For these reasons, many yoga studios do not utilize mirrors, as they are just too distracting. Since yoga encourages self-awareness, many times instructors opt to use verbal, visual, or the occasional hands-on adjustment to teach students how to self-correct for optimal alignment.

When used positively, the mirrors are an excellent resource for checking alignment and ensuring the safe execution of the postures. This works well if you can practice self-control and use them accordingly. For those who have a propensity toward perfectionism or love of self, they can be a hindrance, feeding vanity and ego. Proverbs 16:18 says, "Pride goes before destruction, a haughty spirit before a fall."

Pride indeed comes before a fall for those who harbor it. Some teachers unknowingly exacerbate pride by calling out students by name and telling them how wonderful they look. Whether or not this is the intention, doing so can feed the ego.

For Christians practicing yoga in this environment, it may be tempting to follow suit. On more than one occasion, I have had to keep the focus on my practice and stand firm when others around me consciously or unconsciously stare at themselves. I have been tempted to do the same, to scrutinize myself in poses in my effort to obtain perfection and push myself beyond what I can do physically, all because of pride. When I feel myself going in that direction, I can call on the truth of Romans 12:2: "Do not conform to the pattern of this world, but be transformed by the renewing of your mind. Then you will be able to test and approve what God's will is—his good, pleasing and perfect will." This scripture helps me conquer the temptation to conform and gives me the desire not to cross over into the world of "me" but to stay grounded in humility.

Scripture tells us the heart is deceitful above all else (Jeremiah 17:9). We can apply this to our practice, being mindful that no one is immune to bringing their sin struggles to the mat. Teachers can create judgment or divisiveness simply because they are human and because humans have a propensity to sin. When teachers are not in a relationship with Christ but in a relationship with self, doing so seems apropos to the situation.

Students can become judgmental of themselves and others by letting their looks drive how they practice yoga. Trying to appear "better than" creates a disruption for other students and divides what could be a space of working together and oneness, as is the case with some studios. They can be places to cater to the who's who or the trendy "be seen" crowd. As subtle as these tendencies may seem, remember they reflect the need to be noticed and validated. People want desperately to fit in. In my line of work, for example, I've been expected to look or dress a particular way when working at a specific studio.

Does what you look like in a yoga class matter? Do what you wear and where you practice matter? To some, these things do. People can easily buy into wearing expensive name-brand yoga attire. I have been to studios where everyone looked like they came from a specific brand-name store where the average yoga pants are crazy expensive. If the essence of yoga is not to judge, then is judgment unknowingly fostered by what clothing people choose to wear? For those who can't afford expensive attire, the answer would most likely be affirmative.

Christians are encouraged to be "doers of the word" (James 1:22, ESV). We are called to walk humbly with our God (Micah 6:8), not with an exaggerated sense of self. Humility on the mat can be helpful in overcoming selfishness and vanity because the need to focus obsessively on the body is greatly lessened. When we live in humility, our emphasis is not on perfection, being advanced, or embellishing our bodies with expensive attire. Instead, humility helps us overcome the temptation to think of ourselves more highly than we ought.

How would Jesus respond to people who are less than or don't measure up? He would invite them to come to Him, encouraging and loving them right where they are. Jesus did this repeatedly by surrounding Himself with the most unlikely of characters—His disciples. Isn't "no judgment" really about loving people where they are or, as the Scriptures describe it, "lov[ing] your neighbor as yourself" (Mark 12:31)?

Once we look at the facade of yoga through the lens of truth, it is easy to see the judgment, divisiveness, and unhealthy doses of pride. Perhaps these weaknesses are present because the practice has become so westernized and Western culture thrives on division and the exaltation of self.

How beautiful yoga practice could be if we lived out 1 Thessalonians 5:11, where we are called to "encourage one another and build each other up." The walls of judgment, divisiveness, and self-exaltation would come crashing down. Instead, love, honor, and peace would be the spiritual foundation for encouraging others. Participants would experience the freedom to dress and practice without condemnation and with acceptance.

Scriptural Application

Take a moment to meditate on the truth of God's Word. How can these scriptures help you break free from pride and judgment in yoga practice? How can these verses help you stay connected to God and His truth?

- ❖ "Do not judge by appearances, but judge with right judgment" (John 7:24, ESV).
- ❖ "Don't be selfish; don't try to impress others. Be humble, thinking of others as better than yourselves" (Philippians 2:3, NLT).
- ❖ "Let us stop passing judgment on one another. Instead, make up your mind not to put any stumbling block or obstacle in the way of a brother or sister" (Romans 14:13).
- ❖ "Pride goes before destruction, a haughty spirit before a fall" (Proverbs 16:18).

Call to Action: Write for Insight

- ❖ What are some roots of pride that manifest in your own heart, and would yoga help with these or make them worse?
- ❖ If you currently practice yoga (or desire to), do you struggle (or do you think you would struggle) with being prideful in your practice? Why or why not?
- ❖ Do you think yoga encourages you to try to be competitive or better than others? How do you feel about instructors labeling students as advanced or not advanced? Do you think you would be concerned about what you wore while practicing yoga?
- ❖ What would having a spirit of humility look like for you in a yoga class?

Prayer: *Father God, I thank You for showing me where yoga can exalt my pride. I want to be free from this spirit and view You as the one who is to judge, not me. I hope to embrace a spirit of humility and be a doer of the Word so I can be loving and gracious to those I come in contact with, on or off the mat. In Jesus's name, amen.*

CHAPTER 9

All Meditations Are Not Created Equal

There has been much buzz in the yoga world the last few years about gong meditations, also known as gong ceremonies. I've had different yoga friends describe the gongs as relaxing and positive. Curious but cautious, I decided to experience them myself. This time, before partaking, I put on the full armor of God to guard myself spiritually, as Ephesians 6 encourages.

Upon arrival, I marveled at all the gongs from large to small, both wide and tall. The instructor seemed pleasant, kindly welcoming us. He looked the part in a tie-dyed tee and bell-bottom yoga pants. His long graying hair had been neatly swept back in a partial ponytail, completing his look with John Lennon–style glasses.

We neatly positioned our yoga mats around the gongs and got our blankets and eye pillows to make us comfortable, then settled into a position to relax.

Our instructor explained there would be times when the sounds would be softer and other times when they would be louder. Our part was to stay comfortable and take it all in restoratively. Our guide went on to add, "There may be times when I stand beside certain individuals with the gong and play. If at any time you feel uncomfortable for whatever reason, like the sound is too loud, please feel free to step outside of the room."

Before the class began, I prayed for God to show me anything contradictory to my faith in this type of meditation. The first sound of the gong was super soothing, and I enjoyed the waves of sound quietly washing over me, which allowed my body to peacefully rest.

The instructor walked around the class and periodically stopped in one area. My eyes were covered with an eye pillow, so I tuned in by listening closer. I started to feel somewhat uncomfortable as the sound shifted from serene to intense, hurting my ears at times.

The gong emitted angry sounds, leaving me reeling as all sense of relaxation disappeared. I could sense the gong was on the move, as the sound shifted until it parked itself right alongside me. I removed my eye pillow to peek; the instructor stood beside the woman on my left.

For the next several minutes, he proceeded to bang his gong until the woman started to softly sob. I prayed because

I felt distressed. And when I peeked again and noticed others were leaving, I thought I should too.

As I rolled over on my mat to get up, the gong stopped and the instructor stepped away. The sounds returned to soothing and stayed that way through the remainder of the class. Unfortunately, relaxation eluded me. I felt spiritually on-guard and somewhat troubled as I tried to make sense of what had happened.

Once the teaching was completed, the instructor explained what took place. "When I teach a class, I walk around and read people's energy. I can sense when people need a 'gong bath,' and when they do, I stand beside them and play as soft or loudly as they need until I sense their souls cleansed from negative energy."

That was all I needed to hear to know God was saying a big *no* to gong meditations because the philosophy behind them was rooted in false teaching.

If we are following Christ, we know that when we accept Him as our Savior by confessing our sins and believing in Him, we become spiritually clean. No amount of gonging will ever remove someone's sin; only Jesus can do that.

In 1 John 1:9 we learn that "if we confess our sins, he is faithful and just and will forgive us our sins and purify us from all unrighteousness." Only by having a relationship with Jesus and admitting transgressions to Him can we be cleansed of the soul sickness of sin. Purification of the spirit is a holy transaction, something supernatural between the believer and Jesus. A gong may sound helpful in theory, but it is not rooted in the power of Christ. Instead, it is limited by human power and is therefore unable to cleanse the soul on any level.

The world buys into the lie that people have the power to change their lives and transform their souls—with no need for God, confession of sin, repentance, or heart change. They believe that if you try hard enough, do enough, put works above all else, then total transformation is possible. Yes, transformation (to a degree) is possible, but people can do only so much in their limited power. We need Jesus to make the transformation complete.

In general, the yoga community wholeheartedly buys into the world's view. Society tells us that we have the power to be, think, and feel whatever we want.

Several mantras have been used in training that I have attended as either teacher or student. Mantras originate in Buddhist or Hindu teaching; they are words or statements repeated in meditation—such as "Everything I want is coming to me. I am creating my own successful life. I am powerful."

These thoughts give an illusion that people are solely responsible for their success in life. Chant such phrases over and over, and you are exalting yourself, your ideas, and your ways.

For Christians, this is dangerous thinking, as the scriptures have a different perspective. Proverbs 16:9 says, "The heart of man plans his way, but the Lord establishes his steps" (ESV). You can chant your mantras until your voice is hoarse, but ultimately it is God who decides what course in life is best for you.

Philippians 4:8 provides a better framework for what Christians should ponder when taking a yoga class: "Brothers and sisters, whatever is true, whatever is noble, whatever is right, whatever is pure, whatever is lovely, whatever is admirable—if anything is excellent or praiseworthy—think about such things."

Let's take the same scenario in a Christian-themed yoga class. As the students are resting, preparing for meditation at the end of practice, the instructor begins: "Let's take some deep breaths in and out of our bodies. Let's focus our hearts and our minds on things above, not below. As we breathe in and breathe out, let's focus on gratitude. We work to keep our hearts and our minds focused on thanksgiving and the beauty God has blessed us. Let's thank God for His goodness, His provision for your life, and this truth. Know He is working for your good and on your behalf today. Breathe that in, and let it soak into your soul…"

Notice how a Christian meditation puts the focus on God, His blessings to us, and the goodness that flows from a relationship with Him. If we keep Philippians 4:8 at the forefront of all Christian meditation, then we are focusing on God and the truths of His Word.

Christians are called to think about excellent things, which we must balance with what is right. It is an excellent thought for us to be successful in any way—monetarily, physically, mentally, in business—but the one who brings the success is ultimately not us.

I believe the Philippians verse is a perfect guide to how affirmations can work in a class because it focuses us on spiritual things. In a Christian class, the term *affirmation* is preferred, as we are affirming the truth of God's Word.

Mantras that are rooted in Buddhist ideals exalt self and make us the gods of the universe.

When we think about what is true in a yoga class, we can think about the truth of Christianity, not other religions. When we think about what is noble, we can think about things in God's kingdom. When we think about what is pure, we can think about what is holy. When we think about what is lovely or admirable, we can focus on the attributes of Christ. When we focus on things praiseworthy, we can affirm all the things in our lives that we have to be grateful for because of who God is—making this a realistic, Christ-centered way to approach affirmation when practicing yoga.

The truth is, God is sovereign. His ways are not our ways, so even if we hope, wish, and try to think ourselves into a better life, ultimately, He is the deciding factor. No amount of chanting, gonging, or positive self-thought can elevate you to where you are ordained to be by God.

Scriptural Application

Take a moment to meditate on the truth of God's Word. How can these scriptures shed light on how to find freedom from sin, focus on Christ for success, or think as a Christian? How can these verses apply to yoga and help you stay connected to God and His truth?

❖ "If we confess our sins, he is faithful and just and will forgive us our sins and purify us from all unrighteousness" (1 John 1:9).

❖ "The heart of man plans his way, but the Lord establishes his steps" (Proverbs 16:9, ESV).

❖ "Brothers and sisters, whatever is true, whatever is noble, whatever is right, whatever is pure, whatever is lovely, whatever is admirable—if anything is excellent or praiseworthy—think about such things" (Philippians 4:8).

Call to Action: Write for Insight

❖ Have you ever been part of a New Age practice? How did it make you feel? Do you think such practices are pleasing to God? Do they align with your Christian values or beliefs? Why or why not?

❖ Are you able to differentiate when you are meditating on worldly ideals from when you are meditating on God's truth?

❖ What are the ways you can use Philippians 4:8 today as a framework for your meditation?

❖ If you have used New Age practices or recognize you have focused on yourself in meditation as the source of success or change, take a moment to go before God in prayer, seeking forgiveness. Give God the glory and honor He deserves as the guide in your path of life.

Prayer: *Father God, we acknowledge You as the only one who can heal our brokenness. Forgive us when we look to outside practices that are of no value in making real heart change. May we strive always to keep our minds on things above, namely You, and may we not buy into the worldview that we are the masters of our destinies. In Jesus's name, amen.*

CHAPTER 10

The Gift of Community

I n recent years, having a faith-based studio has led to some interesting observations regarding community. Speaking scripture over students has had an eye-opening and profound effect on people, some of which I never envisioned when God directed me to teach scripturally.

I've had students tell me that my classes make them view various circumstances differently because biblical truth is woven throughout. God's Word will do that to you when you let it take hold of your heart and change your spirit. I find this to be by far the most satisfying word of encouragement anyone could give me as an instructor.

What raises a flag of caution is when students inform me that my classes have become their "church." I make it clear to them, my classes are *not* designed to take the place of communing in the house of the Lord but can be a catalyst for getting them to an actual church. I know my students' feedback is intended to be kind, so I am lovingly firm in my response. My classes create a community feel because God is at the center, creating a spirit of love among those who attend. I believe my classes create a community much like a healthy church would, but the church community has a purpose in the life of a believer that my studio (or any, for that matter) cannot offer.

Thankfully, I have a pertinent illustration of how my yoga community has pointed another to the church community. One of my students—a tall, fit redheaded woman in her sixties—came into my studio and exchanged pleasantries with fellow practitioners as she made her way to her mat. Known for being chatty, she had something she wanted to share with me and some of the other ladies in the class. My heart sings whenever I see my PerfectFit community at its best, as I love the intentionality with which my students encourage one another in their health and practice. This intentionality makes the classes so much more than just exercise because it fosters a sense of comradery.

She started by saying, "I wanted to tell y'all that since I have been coming to Miranda's classes and hearing how she uses scriptures to inspire and challenge us, I have decided it would be good for me to go back to church." She continued, "This is a huge deal for me because I haven't been to church in years, but I realized that when I come here, God speaks to me, and I realized I miss going to church." All of us listening made cheerful sounds of congratulations. Tears surfaced along with a big smile, as I never imagined this would be a benefit for participants when God gave me the vision of my Christian yoga and Pilates studio. I was grateful to be a small part in her plan to reconnect with God and be in the body of believers.

This is the yoga community one would hope for, a community that spurs one another on to love and do good works (Hebrews 10:24), ultimately pointing people back to Christ. Most yoga communities try to foster a sense of belonging, which can be a draw for people who are looking for a place to belong and socialize.

Many people (especially those not walking with Christ) may not know that the desire to be in relationship and community originated when God created Adam and Eve. Genesis 2:18 says, "The Lord God said, 'It is not good that the man should be alone; I will make him a helper fit for him'" (ESV). God saw that man needed a partner, and He created the first human relationship to establish the community of the Lord.

Many Christians practicing yoga can see the importance and value of connecting communally the way God designed. I have witnessed how for others the yoga community is an enticing alternative to a church community because, quite frankly, it is convenient and easier for a variety of reasons. Obviously, secular yoga studios cause concern in this context because Jesus isn't at the core of these communities.

Take a woman I'd seen periodically at a local yoga studio. She was friendly and always immaculately dressed in the latest fashion workout wear. We would smile at each other upon entering the yoga space but nothing beyond that. I felt I had seen her in another social environment but couldn't place it until one day I remembered her face from church. Excited by this, as I am always looking to make connections through Christ in the yoga world, I decided to approach her and introduce myself.

I struck up a conversation, telling her I saw her at church. From that day on, I would weekly seek her out at church to check in and make small talk. Time passed, and I started to see her less frequently at church and came to the realization that she was no longer attending. I genuinely felt concerned, and as it happened that week, I decided to drop into the yoga class where we first engaged.

There she was at her mat, in her usual spot, as I came in. I waved and gradually made my way over to say hello and see how she was doing. I was mindful of being kind and caring as I relayed my concerns about not seeing her at church. She confessed, "I am not going to church for now. My life has gotten so busy with work and family that I don't have the time to go."

I certainly understood those busy seasons myself, and I nodded. "Right now," she proceeded, "I have time to come to yoga, which makes me feel good, so I can be positive about how crazy my life is. It's like my church."

Regardless of whether she was a longtime believer or a baby Christian or someone who did not have a relationship with Jesus, it is a dangerous misconception that going to a yoga class for connection and community is equivalent to going to church—especially because Jesus is often absent in the yoga community. There will often be no biblical truth shared, and there will be no time spent worshipping the one true God as a body of believers or praying or taking communion or studying

God's Word. A traditional yoga class is, however, a prime opportunity to worship oneself.

The concept of community is a wonderful thing, making it crucial to unite yourself to the right one. Where the traditional yoga community falls short is by embracing a worldly perspective—implementing false teaching, exalting self, and drawing your attention away from biblical values. This worldly perspective can exert a slow, subtle pull on your spirit until eventually you are immersed in it, lost and far from God because you desire yoga more than Him.

The Christian community is an essential part of walking with Christ. Community gives support, shares interests and values, and offers a place to retreat to and people to call on when we are in need. Community is enriching and educating, and it validates our belief systems. Romans 12:5 says, "In Christ we, though many, form one body, and each member belongs to all the others." We come together as the body of Christ when we go to church and worship, attend Bible studies, serve, partake in various ministries or missions, and participate in events fostering fellowship.

We make time in our lives for what is important. As my friend said, she no longer had time to go to church but could make the time to go to yoga. If you are making time to attend weekly yoga classes, you may feel pressured at some point to give more of your time. Yoga studios often endorse and upsell a more subtle approach to creating community—what is known as a "yoga challenge."

A yoga challenge can last anywhere from thirty to ninety days, with the primary aim to physically and mentally change you for the better. Consistent attendance is vital, and often roll is taken. The unspoken claim in a yoga challenge is "The more you go, the better you feel," marketing to people who are stressed, fatigued, or out of shape or who need to reset their minds or bodies in some way. Ironically, people joining in on challenges are in poor health because they're already overly committed in their day-to-day lives. The truth is most people's schedules are already too full and can't handle one more thing, and for the Christian trying to juggle it all, how does this affect your spiritual life? You guessed correctly—it suffers!

One close friend claims she can't be in her church community because Sunday is the only day available to regroup from the hectic week, yet she faithfully attends yoga several days a week, *including* Sundays.

Another claim that Christians may believe is "I don't need to go to church anymore because I get my cup filled when I go to yoga."

Truthfully, once you stop going to church and being in the body, it can be hard to make the Christian community a priority again. Deciding to practice yoga rather than being connected to fellow believers reveals what you have chosen in your heart, as the Bible reinforces by stating, "Where your treasure is, there your heart will be also" (Matthew 6:21, ESV).

Some Christians have shunned the church community in favor of the yoga community because they find the "no judgment" mentality to be refreshing. True, the church is full of judgmental people because the church is full of sinners, but the yoga community is the same way. The yoga community will uphold a "no judgment" ideal until you question their teachings or ask about the root of their beliefs.

The yoga community thrives on the worldly view "If it feels good, then do it," a perfect ideal to complement society's instant gratification. People today long to feel good and go to great lengths to achieve that feeling, working hard to avoid pain and seek comfort, not wanting anyone to judge how they attain it.

When does our church community give us instant gratification? Do we walk into the church on Sunday and immediately feel connected to God and His community? Do we have joy and contentment when we go to serve in a particular ministry? Sometimes but not always. There are times when our church community doesn't give us the satisfaction we desire. Sometimes we are doing all the things we are called to do as Christ-followers, and life is still challenging and painful. Why? Quite simply, it's because of sin. We live in a fallen, broken, often disappointing world full of sin, which can be uncomfortable and hard to accept. As sinners, we fall short of the glory of God (Romans 3:23), and our sin separates us from Him. Only Jesus can reconcile us with God if we confess and repent. As we walk in a Christian community, we must uncover and discard sin in our lives. The classes you take at church, the Bible studies you attend, the mentors you have, the ministries you serve in, are all created to help you grow closer to and be more like our holy, loving, supreme God.

The yoga community will never point these truths out to you. The yoga community exalts living for self in efforts to avoid pain and feel good—"Live for your glory, create your best life, and don't let anyone else tell you how to live." None of these ideas are the truth Jesus calls us to live out.

What view should the Christian community take regarding the righteous lives we are called to live? First Corinthians 10:23 says it perfectly: "'I am allowed to do anything'—but not everything is good for you.... 'I am allowed to do anything'— but not everything is beneficial" (NLT). For many reasons, I believe yoga is permissible, but making it your community instead of the church is not beneficial. Yoga is a good thing to have in our lives, but it cannot replace what is best: God and His church.

The body of believers is to die to self and find freedom in walking close to a holy God, whatever the cost. We are to "grow to become in every respect the mature body of him who is the head, that is, Christ" (Ephesians 4:15b). And although you can gain many incredible benefits from practicing in the yoga community, it cannot and will not ever help you grow, mature, and connect to Christ or His body of believers.

Remember, as Jesus tells us in Matthew 7:13–14: "Enter through the narrow gate. For wide is the gate and broad is the road that leads to destruction, and many enter through it. But small is the gate and narrow the road that leads to life, and only a few find it."

Know that the wide gate is the yoga community; it will give you instant pleasure and satisfaction but may pull you away from following Christ, the narrow but life-giving gate!

In all honesty, we may be extremely uncomfortable in our walk with Christ, but He did not call us to live lives of pleasure or comfort. He called us to be obedient and that includes being in the body of Christ, His community.

Relationships are certainly not perfect in God's community. But if they are real and authentically rooted to Christ, they will build you up and call you to live according to a higher standard than the world lives by, which means you have to look at dark, complicated matters of the heart.

It is through the community in Christ that we can experience God's love through our Spirit-born brothers and sisters, a love that is radically different from the love of those who don't follow Him because it is unconditional and has a unique purpose. The purpose is to shape you into the man or woman God created you to be. The yoga community is limited in the type of transformation it can bring because it does not acknowledge the limitless power of an infinite, holy God.

John 15:5 says, "I am the vine; you are the branches. If you remain in me and I in you, you will bear much fruit; apart from me you can do nothing." Make no mistake about it—you must remain in Christ and be the community of believers in order to bear fruit, or you will just be existing in a community with limited growth. The yoga community cannot replace the church community if you are to remain spiritually healthy and rooted in Christ.

Scriptural Application

Take a moment to meditate on the truth of God's Word. How can these scriptures help you view being in God's community as more important than being in the yoga community? If the

Christian community is vital to the believer, how does it look different from the yoga community, according to scripture?

❖ "Speaking the truth in love, we will grow to become in every respect the mature body of him who is the head, that is, Christ" (Ephesians 4:15).

❖ "Enter through the narrow gate. For wide is the gate and broad is the road that leads to destruction, and many enter through it. But small is the gate and narrow the road that leads to life, and only a few find it" (Matthew 7:13–14).

❖ "I am the vine; you are the branches. If you remain in me and I in you, you will bear much fruit; apart from me you can do nothing" (John 15:5).

Call to Action: Write for Insight

❖ If you evaluate your life honestly, do you feel you need to focus more on being part of the Christian community? Why or why not? Are you drawn more to the yoga community than the Christian community? Why or why not?

❖ How do you feel about the Christian community helping you grow into the character of Christ? Do you believe that the yoga community can help you grow in your walk with Christ? Why or why not?

❖ Do you try at all costs to avoid pain or be comfortable in life? Could this be a reason you are drawn to yoga—so you can hear messages encouraging you to live however you choose? How do these messages contradict how God calls you to live?

❖ Do you put more time and effort into being part of the yoga community than the Christian community? If you feel like you want to change in this area, what are some logical steps to redirect your time and effort?

Prayer: *Dear Lord, I know Your community has a purpose and meaning in my life. Please help me want to participate in things that will add value to my walk as a believer. Please help me prioritize my time so I may be a part of Your community. Please show me if I have put yoga and its community ahead of You. If I have, please forgive me, as this is selfish and sinful. Please help me seek first Your kingdom and Your righteousness! In Jesus's name, amen.*

Conclusion

This book recounts my journey in Christ and witnesses to the multitude of ways yoga can challenge believers. By exposing false teachings, this book may have left you wondering whether it is safe for Christians to be *in* the yoga world but not *of* it.

Hopefully, the scriptural truths and action items at the end of each chapter bring greater clarity and insight to your personal yoga journey so you can confidently know how God is guiding you in the practice.

With the right precautions, Christians can adapt yoga to make it God-centered.

Let's take a look at some questions worth asking:

- ❖ How can Christians safely practice yoga?
- ❖ How do I find a Christian yoga instructor?
- ❖ Are there yoga studios or styles of yoga that emphasize movement and not philosophy?

The "how-to" factor is hugely relevant for Christians. Participating in the yoga world requires biblical wisdom, discernment, and prayer. We want classes that will speak of the mental and physical benefits but not compromise our Christian faith.

For these reasons, I strongly encourage you to take advantage of my complimentary action guide, "How to Practice Yoga and Not Compromise Your Faith." This step-by-step guide highlights the top three tips from my next book aiming to direct Christians in their search for the ideal yoga studio, instructor, or class. My simple format gives any potential practitioner vital information to successfully discern how to proceed and partake in the practice.

Let's unite as children of the light and boldly step out in faith to enjoy yoga within God-given parameters and with His guidance. *All* things are possible with Him, including yoga. May we all experience His favor, grace, and bountiful blessing as we courageously shine for Christ every time we step onto the mat and into the yoga world.

Acknowledgments

For the unconditional love and support of my husband, Erich, and my two boys, Joah and Levi. I am so thankful for your encouragement during this journey.

Thank you to my editors, Susan Tjaden, Eva Marie Everson, Kayla Fenstermaker, and Mikaela Mathews.

Thank you, Alisa Hope Wagner, for helping me get started in the right direction with my writing.

Thank you to Self-Publishing School for teaching me all I needed to know to successfully self-publish a book.

Thank you to all my students who have supported me in teaching Christian yoga over the years. I love you all and am so glad we have created a special community.

I am grateful to my church home, Christ Chapel in Fort Worth, Texas, for giving me solid biblical knowledge so I have a firm foundation in God's truth.

Photography credit: Roland Moriarty and Brian Hutson.

Notes

1   "What Does It Mean to Be a RYT?," Yoga Alliance,
    accessed February 18, 2020, www.yogaalliance.org/
    Become_a_Member/Member_Overview/RYT_
    Resource_Center/What_Does_It_Mean_To_Be_a_RYT.

2   Yoga Alliance, accessed February 18, 2020,
    www.yogaalliance.org.

3   "Yoga's Benefits from Head to Toe," Johns Hopkins Medicine,
    accessed February 19, 2020, www.hopkinsmedicine.org/health/
    wellness-and-prevention/yogas-benefits-from-head-to-toe.

4   "What Is Tantra?," Institute of Authentic Tantra
    Education, accessed February 19, 2020, www.
    authentictantra.com/about-tantra.

5   "Power Yoga," *Yoga Journal*, accessed February 19, 2020,
    www.yogajournal.com/yoga-101/types-of-yoga/
    power-types-of-yoga.

6   *2016 Yoga in America Study* (*Yoga Journal* and Yoga
    Alliance, 2016), 4, www.yogaalliance.org/Portals/
    0/2016%20Yoga%20in%20America%20
    Study%20RESULTS.pdf.

7   Das Goravani, "What Is Vedic Hindu Astrology?,"
    Learn Religions, last modified April 10, 2019, www.
    learnreligions.com/what-is-vedic-astrology-1770025.

8   "The Vedas," Yoga Basics, accessed February 19,
    2020, www.yogabasics.com/learn/the-vedas.

9   Nora Isaacs, "What Is Bhakti Yoga? Why You Should
    Try the Yoga of Devotion," *Yoga Journal*, July 16, 2008,
    www.yogajournal.com/yoga-101/bhakti-yoga-love-
    devotion-relationship.

10 "How to Practice Karma Yoga: Principles and Benefits," Yoga
    Institute, accessed February 19, 2020, https://
    theyogainstitute.org/karma-yoga-practice-principles-
    benefits.

11 Lexico, s.v. "worship," accessed February 19, 2020,
    www.lexico.com/en/definition/worship.

12 Ned Herrmann, "What Is the Function of the Various
    Brainwaves?," *Scientific American*, December 22, 1997,
    www.scientificamerican.com/article/what-is-the-function-
    of-t-1997-12-22; "Brain Waves and Meditation,"
    Science Daily, March 31, 2010, www.sciencedaily.
    com/releases/2010/03/100319210631.htm.

13 "Yoga Sutra," *Yoga Journal*, accessed February 20, 2020,
    www.yogajournal.com/yoga-101/philosophy/yoga-sutras.

About the Author

Miranda Jo Davis is an expert in the health and wellness world with over twenty years' experience. She owns a thriving Christian yoga and Pilates studio and infuses her teaching with biblical truth. Miranda facilitates global wellness retreats, has an E-RYT 500 credential from Yoga Alliance, and has made several television, radio, and print appearances as a top resource.

In ministry, Miranda is a biblical counselor, using God's Word to encourage heart change and guide women to live for Christ. She has a heart for marriage and serves alongside her husband, Erich, by mentoring couples in need.

As a freelance writer and blogger, she has written devotionals, blogs, and articles for various Christian media outlets such as Proverbs 31 Ministries. Miranda routinely does public speaking and has a love for sharing God's Word, using personal testimony on a variety of topics to convey the impact Christ has on her life.

Despite Miranda's passion for investing in others, her family is her top priority. Her husband is her best friend, with whom she lovingly parents two boys, Joah and Levi. Together they find the joy in life by being outdoors, traveling, eating great food, laughing a lot, and dancing to music that moves the soul.

HOW CAN YOU

Help?

I am so grateful you read my book! I truly appreciate your feedback, and I love hearing what you have to say. I need your input to make the next version of this book and my future books better. Please leave me an honest review on Amazon letting me know what you thought of the book. Thank you!

Abundant blessings,
Miranda Jo Davis